LiFE

LiFE

A TEEN DEVOTIONAL

Words from the Rock

MELODY CARLSON

Revell

a division of Baker Publishing Group
Grand Rapids, Michigan

Published by Revell
a division of Baker Publishing Group
P.O. Box 6287, Grand Rapids, MI 49516-6287
www.revellbooks.com

Printed in the United States of America

Library of Congress Cataloging-in-Publication Data
Carlson, Melody.
    Life : a teen devotional / Melody Carlson.
      p.   cm. — (Words from the rock ; bk. 2)
    ISBN 978-0-8007-3255-4 (pbk.)
    1. Christian teenagers—Prayers and devotions. 2. Bible. N. T. Matthew—Meditations. 3. Bible N. T. John—Meditations. I. Title.
    BV4850.C333 2009
    242'.63—dc22   2009017719

Contents

Introduction

I didn't grow up in a traditional churchgoing home. In fact, I proclaimed myself an atheist at the ripe old age of twelve. For some reason it made sense to me—I saw no signs of God and therefore thought he couldn't possibly exist. I think I secretly hoped he'd straighten me out. Thankfully, by the time I was fifteen, he did. In the course of one week, I did a 180-degree turnaround from a loud-mouthed atheist to a sold-out believer.

I didn't know a thing about the Bible, and I had no idea where to begin. So I just started reading and studying and memorizing Scripture. I must have been trying to make up for lost time, since my new Christian friends already seemed to know a lot about the Bible. My goal was to absorb as much Scripture as I possibly could. And for years that's just what I did.

Then one day, I noticed that I felt totally satiated—like a person who'd sat at the table for too long on Thanksgiving. So I literally went on a Bible fast—I put my Bible in a drawer and didn't open it. Not that I'd recommend this to everyone, but it seemed to be just what I needed.

After a while, I knew it was it was time to read my Bible again, but I wanted to do something different. This time I decided to focus only on the words of Jesus. I got a red-letter Bible (in which all of Jesus's words are printed in red) and read only the red words. And it was awesome. I realized that Jesus's words truly were words of life—and they were just the words my life needed.

My hope is that you'll experience that same kind of life as you read these devotionals—the kind of life that comes straight from the only one who can give you real life, the one who wants to be your lifeline. Jesus is the way, the truth, and the LIFE.

1

Birdseed Faith

Words from the Rock

A farmer went out to sow his seed. As he was scattering the seed, some fell along the path, and the birds came and ate it up.

Matthew 13:3–4 NIV

Jesus told this parable to a crowd at the lake one day. Jesus often used parables, which are actually stories, to teach critical life lessons—probably because he knew we'd do better recalling a story than a boring twelve-part lecture. He also understood that most listeners wouldn't fully grasp the meaning of the story the first time they heard it, but perhaps over time (as it's told again and again), the truth would sink in.

The soil in this story represents our hearts. In other words, Jesus compares our hearts to dirt. (Before you get offended, remember that God formed humans from the earth.) The seed in this story represents the gospel—the Good News that Jesus was God's Son sent to earth to offer humankind a new and improved relationship with God. Unfortunately, not all who hear this Good News will take it seriously, and that explains this parable.

The reaction of some listeners is like a tough old road. The seed lands on the hard-packed dirt and then just sits there because it can't penetrate the hardened surface of a well-traveled road. It's as if the road rejects it. Kind of like people with hardened hearts or heads. They're unwilling to listen, simply rejecting the Good News as soon as it hits them. It almost seems that the seed is wasted. In fact, Jesus adds that the birds come and eat it—the precious Good News is nothing more than worthless birdseed to them.

Maybe we don't think we fall into this birdseed kind of faith category, but there are times when anyone can be a little hard-hearted—times when we might choose to disobey God or reject a truth he's shown us. Jesus doesn't want us to treat his words like birdseed. He wants hearts that are softened and ready to welcome his Good News, allow it to grow, and make strong roots.

My Prayer

Dear God,
Please keep my heart plowed and tilled (with your Word and your truth) so that, unlike birdseed, my faith will root deeply into you.
Amen.

Stone
for the Journey

I won't allow myself to become hard-hearted toward God.

Final Word

When anyone hears the message about the kingdom and does not understand it, the evil one comes and snatches away what was sown in his heart. This is the seed sown along the path.

Matthew 13:19 NIV

Tumbleweed Faith

Words from the Rock

Some [seed] fell on rocky places, where it did not have much soil. It sprang up quickly, because the soil was shallow. But when the sun came up, the plants were scorched, and they withered because they had no root.

Matthew 13:5–6 NIV

*N*ow Jesus is talking about another kind of farming challenge. This particular seed (still representing Jesus's Good News) fell onto rocky places—ground that hasn't been plowed, cultivated, or prepared for agriculture. It's probably rough, uneven, full of stones, and basically not the kind of soil to grow much of anything (besides tumbleweed, which can be here one day and gone the next).

This rocky ground represents those with a willingness to hear the Good News. They might even experience a positive reaction to it—initially—but that's about all. They haven't reached the place in life where they want to take God's words and promises seriously, so they adopt a kind of fair-weather faith. Maybe they say, "Yeah, I know Jesus is real and he cares about me, and that's cool," but they don't grasp the hugeness of a relationship with God. For them, faith is more like a fad—when temptations or tough times come, they let their faith slip away like last year's fashion trends.

These people are similar to a plant that grows up without a strong root system. Their seed gets wedged between a rock and a hard place with little real soil—following a gentle spring rain, the plant pops up and might even seem healthy for a while. But then a few hot, sunny days come along, and because the plant doesn't have real roots, it simply dries up and blows away, kind of like tumbleweed. Those people who make a showy commitment to Christ but don't really take it seriously can spiritually dry up and blow away too.

Jesus wants us to have healthy and established roots that go deeply into him to strengthen our faith. Then we can grow and flourish even during drought times.

My Prayer

Dear God,
Please help me to establish strong roots in you so I can withstand whatever storms or droughts life throws my way.
Amen.

Stone
for the Journey

**I will root
myself deeply
into God.**

Final Word

The one who received the seed that fell on rocky places is the man who hears the word and at once receives it with joy. But since he has no root, he lasts only a short time. When trouble or persecution comes because of the word, he quickly falls away.

Matthew 13:20–21 NIV

3

Weedy Faith

> *Other seed fell among thorns, which grew up and choked the plants.*
>
> Matthew 13:7 NIV

*T*his third category in this seed parable is interesting. From what we can tell, this seed has fallen on some fairly good soil because it actually grows into a plant. The only problem is that there are weeds and thorns growing in this same patch of ground. The trouble with weeds and thorns is that they hog the water, the sun, and the nutrients in the soil, and they can eventually take over and choke out an otherwise healthy plant.

This weed-infested garden represents those who hear Jesus's Good News and willingly receive it. They happily plant the seed into their hearts, where the soil seems nicely plowed and ready for cultivation, and the seed develops roots and grows. Everything is cool, right? Except that the plant isn't the only thing growing there. Sure, those itty-bitty weeds may not look terribly threatening at first. Maybe they even resemble flowers. But weeds left to grow will get out of control and eventually ruin the garden.

Weeds and thorns are symbols for sin. Like weeds that take over a garden, sin can take over our hearts. We need to confess our sin to God and receive his forgiveness, but that's not all. Just like a farmer who diligently pulls weeds from the field, God wants to uproot sin from our lives. He knows that when we neglect those weeds and continue doing what we know is wrong, the weeds will take over and possibly choke out our faith completely.

My Prayer

Dear God,
Thank you for your forgiveness. I know that sin is as common as weeds, but please help me to deal with it on a daily basis.
Amen.

Stone
for the Journey

I will not allow sin to crowd out my faith.

Final Word

The one who received the seed that fell among the thorns is the man who hears the word, but the worries of this life and the deceitfulness of wealth choke it, making it unfruitful.

Matthew 13:22 NIV

4

Amazing Faith!

Words from the Rock

> *Some [seed] fell on good earth, and produced a*
> *harvest beyond [the farmer's] wildest dreams. Are*
> *you listening to this? Really listening?*
>
> Matthew 13:8–9 Message

*A*t the end of Jesus's parable about the challenges of planting seeds, we finally get to hear about the seeds that not only survived but flourished and thrived. Jesus simply says, "Some fell on good earth." But what does that mean? What makes earth good?

Jesus begins this parable by saying that a farmer went out to sow some seed. Now if you ask an experienced farmer about the best way to plant a successful crop, he'll immediately give you the lowdown on field preparation. He'll suggest nutrients and explain the importance of plowing and turning the soil. And he'll definitely point out that timing is everything.

So what do our hearts have in common with dirt? For starters, we need to be plowed (another word for *plowing* is *breaking* the soil), and that can be painful. Sometimes it's when life knocks us around and beats us up that we become ready to hear and receive

God's Good News. It's like the hard times have plowed through and softened our hearts.

There's also the matter of timing. Only a foolish farmer would try to plant seeds in hard, frozen earth, but a freezing-cold winter also helps to break up and prepare the soil for planting. Kind of like when we go through a season that feels like winter—it could be preparing our hearts. Then spring comes, and like soil that's warm and soft, our hearts are ready to receive a seed. The timing is right, seeds are planted, the soil is fertile, plants appear, and in due time—a harvest!

Jesus describes this harvest as beyond a farmer's wildest dreams. What Jesus means is that this is just the beginning, because when his seeds of faith grow strong and healthy in us, we can't help but produce more seeds that we share with others, and the crop of faith gets bigger and bigger.

At the end of this parable, Jesus urgently asks, "Are you listening? Can you hear what I'm telling you?" This message is vital, so he wants us to really get it.

My Prayer

Dear God,
I want my heart to be plowed and ready to receive your seed of faith. Help me to be patient if it feels painful or it feels like I'm stuck in winter. I trust your timing.
Amen.

Final Word

> But the one who received the seed that
> fell on good soil is the man who hears the word
> and understands it. He produces a crop, yielding a
> hundred, sixty or thirty times what was sown.
>
> Matthew 13:23 NIV

Stone
for the Journey

I submit my heart to God's plow so I will be ready to receive his faith seeds.

5
Puzzle Pieces

Words from the Rock

I have explained the secrets about the kingdom of heaven to you, but not to others. Everyone who has something will be given more. But people who don't have anything will lose even what little they have. I use stories when I speak to them because when they look, they cannot see, and when they listen, they cannot hear or understand.

Matthew 13:11–13 CEV

*J*esus is responding to his disciples' question about why he so often used stories to teach people. First he reminds them that he's disclosed to them almost everything regarding faith and God already. Jesus's reasoning is that these twelve men, chosen by him, are capable of grasping some deep spiritual truths. In fact, that's why he chose them. At the same time, he knows that others aren't quite so ready—not yet.

Jesus knew that most of his listeners wouldn't really get the depth of his messages. That's because he was introducing what was about to begin a major revolution in religion—it would change everything!

So he used stories in order to give his listeners a little something to hold on to for later. He knew that people are good at remembering and retelling stories. Even if they didn't get the real spiritual meaning in the story right away, they would recall the story later, and eventually the truth would sink in.

That's why he says that those who have something will be given more. It's like we all receive some pieces of this faith puzzle, and even if they don't seem to work or fit at first, they will eventually make perfect sense. In other words, none of us gets the whole picture of what God is up to right from the start. It's a process of living, learning, and experiencing God as we continue to follow his will, and as he makes himself known to us more and more.

My Prayer

Dear God,
Help me to understand that I can't possibly grasp all spiritual meanings right from the start. Help me to be patient and persistent as I get to know you better each day.
Amen.

Stone
for the Journey

I believe God will provide the spiritual truth I need for this day.

Final Word

Jesus used stories to tell all these things to the people; he always used stories to teach them. This is as the prophet said: "I will speak using stories; I will tell things that have been secret since the world was made."

Matthew 13:34–35 NCV

6

Enemy Seeds

Words from the Rock

The kingdom of heaven is like what happened when a farmer scattered good seed in a field. But while everyone was sleeping, an enemy came and scattered weed seeds in the field and then left.

When the plants came up and began to ripen, the farmer's servants could see the weeds. The servants came and asked, "Sir, didn't you scatter good seed in your field? Where did these weeds come from?"

"An enemy did this," he replied.

Matthew 13:24–28 CEV

*J*esus is using another agricultural metaphor—more seeds and planting and weeds. But this story takes a different twist. This time the seeds represent the lives of believers—believers who were carefully planted by Jesus in a field ready for cultivation. The field represents the world we live in—a world where anything can happen, a place where good and evil cohabitate and sometimes collide. The weeds represent those who try to destroy the faith of believers. And Jesus states clearly that the weeds are not planted by him; they are planted by the enemy.

Jesus understands the frustrations of trying to be a strong Christian while evil influences push in from all sides—kind of like those obnoxious weeds crowding in. He knows what we're up against. Whether it's sleazy things we see or hear or the way someone mistreats us, Jesus realizes that it's not easy being a Christian and that it can be a challenge to consistently make good choices. Although we have control over our own actions, we can't control what others do. We can't prevent weeds (evil) from cropping up next door.

Fortunately, Jesus has a strategy for dealing with the weeds all around us, and he has a plan to rescue us. Mostly we just need to sink our roots into him and trust his timing.

My Prayer

Dear God,
I see that, like weeds, evil is alive and well on planet earth. Help me to root myself deeply into you so you can protect me.
Amen.

Stone
for the Journey

I trust that
God will deal
with the evil
in this world.

Final Word

The one who sowed the good seed is the Son of Man. The field is the world, and the good seed stands for the sons of the kingdom. The weeds are the sons of the evil one, and the enemy who sows them is the devil. The harvest is the end of the age, and the harvesters are angels.

Matthew 13:37–39 NIV

7

In Due Time

Words from the Rock

His servants then asked, "Do you want us to go out and pull up the weeds?"

"No!" he answered. "You might also pull up the wheat. Leave the weeds alone until harvest time. Then I'll tell my workers to gather the weeds and tie them up and burn them. But I'll have them store the wheat in my barn."

Matthew 13:28–30 CEV

The farmer's servants are asking if they should go out and weed the field. Knowing that weeds are generally bad news, we expect the farmer to say, "Yeah, get rid of those weeds, and hurry it up." But his answer is an emphatic *no!*

He explains that pulling up the weeds will harm the young wheat plants. This suggests that the infestation of weeds is extremely severe—that the weeds are so prolific and so entrenched into the soil that they might destroy the wheat if they're pulled up.

Now remember that the seeds (in this case seedling plants) represent believers and the weeds represent evil. So what Jesus is really saying is that there is so much evil, and it's such a big part of this world, that it's impossible to get rid of all of the evil without getting rid of everything. In other words, he's saying that we have to endure it—that evil is simply a part of living in this world.

Does that mean we give in and let the weeds (evil) take over our lives? Of course not. Jesus wants us to have strong roots and to grow up healthy and whole. He wants us to hang in there until it's time for him to finally remove the weeds (destroying evil once and for all), to rescue his believers, and to reward them with heaven—where no weeds are allowed!

My Prayer

Dear God,
I look forward to the day when I will be free from the influence of evil. In the meantime, teach me how to be strong and stand up against it.
Amen.

Stone
for the Journey

I trust God's plan and timing to eradicate evil from this world.

Final Word

The picture of thistles pulled up and burned is a scene from the final act. The Son of Man will send his angels, weed out the thistles from his kingdom, pitch them in the trash, and be done with them.

Matthew 13:40–41 Message

8

Small Beginnings

Words from the Rock

God's kingdom is like a pine nut that a farmer plants. It is quite small as seeds go, but in the course of years it grows into a huge pine tree, and eagles build nests in it.

Matthew 13:31–32 Message

Most versions of the Bible call this the mustard seed faith parable. But the Message uses a pine nut to describe faith. If you've ever made pesto sauce, you know that a pine nut is pretty small (and tasty). Yet it's capable of growing into an enormous tree.

If you think about it—really consider the fact that the insignificant pine nut contains the "magical" ingredients to transform itself into a towering pine tree—it's nothing short of miraculous. That is exactly the way Jesus describes faith in God's kingdom. It starts out small, then grows into the biggest thing imaginable.

Think about your own life. Do you remember when you first put your trust in God? How big was your faith compared to the size of God's kingdom? Did it resemble an insignificant pine nut next to a majestic pine tree? Or maybe you haven't even taken that step yet. Maybe your faith seems impossibly small and you're fairly certain it could never grow into anything. But if you have just that tiny bit of faith, and if you plant that faith by asking Jesus to come into your life and to begin building his kingdom inside your heart, it will grow.

Most people come to God with all sorts of doubts and questions, and their faith feels puny and weak at first. But over time, and with God's help, faith grows, and eventually it's transformed into the most enormous thing in the universe—God's kingdom.

My Prayer

Dear God,
Help me to recognize the huge potential that you've planted inside of me—my faith in you and your kingdom! Help my faith to grow and to strengthen.
Amen.

Stone
for the Journey

My faith in God's kingdom is growing daily.

Final Word

Faith is the assurance of things hoped for, the conviction of things not seen.

Hebrews 11:1 NASB

9

Major Minors

Words from the Rock

God's kingdom is like yeast that a woman works into the dough for dozens of loaves of barley bread—and waits while the dough rises.

Matthew 13:33 Message

Most people don't give something like yeast much thought. It seems like a pretty minor baking ingredient, and it comes in small packages. But again, this "insignificant" substance has the power to increase and transform something else.

It seems slightly ironic that Jesus used so many "minor" elements to teach major lessons. But consider Jesus's coming to earth. It was as if God wanted to make a point by using what seemed small and unimportant—in fact, a tiny, helpless baby—to do something so enormous that it changed the world forever. Yet for most people who lived then, it seemed like no big deal.

At the same time in history, many religions relied on flashy, splashy, huge, over-the-top kinds of gimmicks to persuade worshipers to follow them. Enormous golden idols and ornate buildings were the norm—anything to impress and draw attention. But those religions were all show and no go. The way Jesus got people's attention was simply through his presence. He spoke and they listened. He did miracles and they watched. He was only one man, and he had no ornate temple, no golden statues, no splashy clothes, no flashy musicians—he was so *not* Las Vegas. In fact, he probably seemed fairly minor when he started his ministry. Not only did people not give him much attention, many of them put him down as a nobody. They said nothing good could come from his hometown.

Early on, Jesus got about as much respect as a tiny seed or a flake of yeast, yet he was God's own Son, and his relatively short life on earth would transform the world. In the same way, he wants to have an impact on our lives. When Jesus begins a relationship with us, the changes in our lives might seem minor, but as we get to know him better, he transforms us into people who are able to do major things.

My Prayer

Dear God,
Help me to nurture what may seem like minor things in my life. Acts of kindness, truths quietly shared, unrewarded generosity . . . small things that transform lives.
Amen.

Stone
for the Journey

Jesus at work in me can accomplish major things.

Final Word

The people were upset with Jesus. But Jesus said to them, "A prophet is honored everywhere except in his hometown and in his own home." So he did not do many miracles there because they had no faith.

Matthew 13:57–58 NCV

10

Secret Treasure

Words from the Rock

The kingdom of heaven is like what happens when someone finds a treasure hidden in a field and buries it again. A person like that is happy and goes and sells everything in order to buy that field.

Matthew 13:44 CEV

Did you ever dream of finding an ancient treasure map when you were a kid? Or maybe you dug a big hole at the beach hoping that you'd stumble across some pirate's hidden trunk of gold and jewels? Almost every kid has fantasized about things like that. In fact, millions of grown-ups buy lottery tickets every day just hoping to strike it rich.

When Jesus tells this parable, you can imagine how some of his listeners' eyes light up when he mentions a secret treasure hidden in a field. Maybe they even wonder if he actually knew of such a field. Of course, he isn't talking about a physical treasure—something that would be here today and gone tomorrow. He's talking about himself. He's like a treasure—an everlasting treasure that can do more to transform your life than billions of dollars.

Jesus is saying that it's worthwhile to devote all of your attention to getting this treasure. Just like the person who sells all he owns to buy the field that contains the treasure, you'll never be sorry if you invest all of yourself into knowing and following Jesus. The riches he brings to your life (love, forgiveness, hope, peace) will far outweigh any sacrifices you made.

Do you understand the value of what Jesus is offering you? Do you know its worth? How much have you invested so far? How much are you willing to invest?

My Prayer

Dear God,
Help me to understand the enormity of what you have for me. Show me ways I can invest more of myself into experiencing more of you in my life.
Amen.

> # Stone
> *for the Journey*
>
> **I will invest my whole heart into knowing Jesus better.**

Final Word

You cannot serve two masters: God and money. For you will hate one and love the other, or else the other way around.

Matthew 6:24 TLB

11

What Cost?

Words from the Rock

Again, the kingdom of heaven is like a merchant looking for fine pearls. When he found one of great value, he went away and sold everything he had and bought it.

Matthew 13:45–46 NIV

Salvation is free, right? Or is it? We know that we can't write a check and purchase our faith. We know that anyone who tries to get us to open our wallets and pull out some money to purchase God's forgiveness is a fraud. Yet Jesus is telling another story about the cost of something. What does it mean?

In this parable a man is searching for valuable pearls. He finds a single one that's so exquisite, so valuable, he can hardly believe it. Unfortunately, he doesn't have enough money to buy such an incredible pearl. So he goes off and sells all he owns just so he can come back and purchase that perfect pearl.

Okay, we already know that the perfect pearl represents Jesus and God's kingdom. But the fact that Jesus is repeating parables like this (first the one about the treasure in the field, and now this one) suggests that this is extremely important. He wants us to get it.

Jesus is telling us to invest ourselves completely into our faith. No holding back. No cheapskates allowed. Maybe it's because he knows that we get what we pay for—in this case, spending all we have in order to receive all we need. And if we consider our "everything" (which isn't much) compared to God's "everything" (which is beyond what we can imagine) . . . well, he's only offering the best deal on the planet. So why hold anything back?

My Prayer

Dear God,
Help me to get this, to wrap my head around the fact that you want me to give everything so you can give everything back.
Amen.

Final Word

For where your treasure is, there your heart will be also.

Matthew 6:21 NIV

Stone
for the Journey

I am willing to pour out all I have to receive all God has for me.

12

Finders Keepers

Words from the Rock

> God's kingdom is like a fishnet cast into the sea, catching all kinds of fish. When it is full, it is hauled onto the beach. The good fish are picked out and put in a tub; those unfit to eat are thrown away. That's how it will be when the curtain comes down on history. The angels will come and cull the bad fish and throw them in the garbage. There will be a lot of desperate complaining, but it won't do any good.
>
> Matthew 13:47–50 Message

Most people don't really want to think about the end times. The term sounds pretty ominous and, well, final. But the interesting thing about the end times is that it happens in *everyone's* lifetime—everyone's life will end eventually. It's inevitable. So make no mistake, you will see the end times—someday.

So maybe you're wondering what throwing out fish has to do with the end times. In some ways, this story seems similar to the one about the weeds growing in the grain field, where everything is harvested together but the weeds are thrown away. Likewise, in this metaphor, all the fish (representing people) are gathered up together. The net is cast into the sea, catching all kinds of fish—the good, the bad, and the ugly. Naturally, the fisherman hopes that all the fish caught in the net will be keepers. A good fisherman doesn't want to throw anything back. Neither does Jesus.

In fact, Jesus gives everyone the same invitation to believe and follow him. It's just that some reject that invitation. Again and again some will stubbornly refuse. Although Jesus never stops trying to get people to accept him, there comes a time (the end time) when the net is cast and the final decision is just that—final.

Of course, Jesus is the only one who knows which "fish" are keepers and which ones will get tossed—and there are sure to be a lot of surprises in heaven because, knowing Jesus, he'll probably give some of those stubborn fish one last chance to change their minds. Still, why would you want to wait until the last minute when you could be enjoying a relationship with Jesus for your entire life?

My Prayer

Dear God,
I reaffirm my faith in you. I don't want to be like the fish that's tossed aside. Keep me safe in your net.
Amen.

Stone
for the Journey

I will serve Jesus until the end of time.

Final Word

If anyone loves God, this one is known by Him.

1 Corinthians 8:3 NKJV

13

Equipped and Ready

Words from the Rock

*Every student of the Scriptures who becomes a disciple
in the kingdom of heaven is like someone who brings out
new and old treasures from the storeroom.*

Matthew 13:52 CEV

Jesus has just done a spot-check with his disciples by asking if they're really getting what he's been telling them mostly in parables. They assure him that they have a handle on it, which must be a relief to him because he has so much more to teach them, and a relatively short time to do it.

But he takes a moment to encourage them. He reminds them of the fact that they've been well trained in Judaism. These guys grew up attending synagogue, studying Jewish laws, and learning about the prophets. It was a good foundation for the new things Jesus was now teaching them. Their prior education was important because it wouldn't be long before these same men would be teaching others and building the first Christian church.

Jesus says that this kind of preparation—of having old teaching combined with new—is like being a wealthy homeowner or shopkeeper, a person with all kinds of materials available and ready. Whether he has a valuable antique he can trade or something modern and useful, this person will be well equipped and ready for anything.

That's what Jesus wants for us too. He wants us to understand his words and his teachings and to appreciate how they change our lives so that we too can be ready and equipped for whatever might come our way.

My Prayer

Dear God,
Help me to commit to spending more time reading your Word, learning about you, and making your teaching a vital part of my life. Amen.

Stone
for the Journey

I will take time to know God better.

Final Word

If they listen and obey God, they will be blessed with prosperity throughout their lives. All their years will be pleasant.

Job 36:11 NLT

14

Miracle Meal

Words from the Rock

The disciples came to [Jesus] and said, ". . . Send the crowds away so they can go to the villages and buy food for themselves."

But Jesus said, "That isn't necessary—you feed them."

"But we have only five loaves of bread and two fish!" they answered.

"Bring them here," he said. Then he told the people to sit down on the grass. Jesus took the five loaves and two fish, looked up toward heaven, and blessed them. Then, breaking the loaves into pieces, he gave the bread to the disciples, who distributed it to the people. . . . About 5,000 men were fed that day, in addition to all the women and children!

Matthew 14:15–19, 21 NLT

Jesus has just heard the disturbing news that his cousin John the Baptist was brutally murdered. In need of some serious downtime, Jesus travels by boat to a remote place. But as it turns out, thousands of fans follow him to that out-of-the-way spot, and instead of spending time alone, Jesus spends the entire day helping and healing people. Suddenly everyone begins to get hungry, but because they're out in the sticks, there's no handy place to get food. No McDonald's, no convenience mart, not even a produce stand. Nothing.

So what does Jesus say when his disciples suggest that he send the crowds home so they can eat? He says that's not necessary, and he tells his disciples, "You feed them." Can't you just see their confused expressions? How are they supposed to feed thousands when all they have are five small loaves of bread and two fish? It's barely enough to feed just a few people. What does Jesus expect them to do?

Jesus expects them to have faith. In fact, one of the reasons he does miracles like this is to increase their faith. So he takes the bit of food they have, holds it up, and asks God to bless it. Then he tells his disciples to hand it out to the thousands of people. Imagine how stunned they must have been when not only did they have enough to feed the thousands, but after everyone was thoroughly stuffed, there were twelve large baskets of leftovers!

How do you react when Jesus asks you to do what seems impossible? Maybe he wants you to be kind to someone you can't stand—so you ask for his help, and he empowers you to do it. Or perhaps it feels bigger, like needing God to provide you with college tuition money—and trusting he'll do it. The point is, he wants you to remember that he's the one who will actually perform the miracle. You only need to believe him and obey.

My Prayer

Dear God,
Thank you for reminding me that you're able to do miracles in my life. Help me to increase my faith by being obedient to your will.
Amen.

Final Word

> Those who know your name trust in you, for you, O Lord, do not abandon those who search for you.
>
> Psalm 9:10 NLT

Stone
for the Journey

I will believe that God can work a miracle in my life today.

15

Fearless Faith

Words from the Rock

At once, Jesus said to them, "Don't worry! I am Jesus. Don't be afraid."

Matthew 14:27 CEV

*J*esus's disciples are freaking out when Jesus says these words to them. Ironically, this takes place shortly after Jesus's miracle of feeding the thousands. Jesus has sent the disciples out in a boat when a huge squall breaks out. If you've ever been on a small boat during a big storm, you might understand why they're so frightened—the wind is whipping tall waves right over their boat, and it doesn't look good. Perhaps the disciples wonder why Jesus sent them out in this kind of weather. Doesn't he care about them?

Then suddenly they spot someone walking toward them—on the water! At first they think it's a ghost, and they're even more terrified. Maybe they think it's the Grim Reaper coming for them. Then the man on the water calls out to them and tells them not to be afraid. It's Jesus! Peter yells back at him, "Lord, if it is really you, tell me to come to you on the water" (v. 28 CEV). Jesus tells Peter to come, and suddenly Peter is walking on the water too. But then he takes his eyes off Jesus and focuses on the wind and the waves. He starts to sink, crying out to Jesus for help. Jesus takes his hand, steadying him, and then tells Peter that he doesn't have much faith.

Peter had enough faith to climb out of that boat and walk on the water. He was really trusting Jesus in that moment. But when he took his eyes off Jesus and focused on what was going on around him (the wind, the waves, and *walking on water*), he got scared.

That can happen to you too. You might be in a tough spot, yet you believe that God is helping you and it's going to be okay. Then suddenly you take your eyes off God and stare at what's going on around you, and your faith fades and you begin to go down. God wants you to have fearless faith—the kind of faith where you keep your eyes on him and know he can get you through anything.

My Prayer

Dear God,
Help me to be faithful to keep my eyes on you and what you're doing in my life. Remind me that if I feel like I'm sinking, I can still call out to you for help and you'll answer.
Amen.

Final Word

> *I love everyone who loves me, and I will be found by all who honestly search.*
>
> Proverbs 8:17 CEV

Stone
for the Journey

I will keep my eyes on God and believe he can get me through anything.

16

Fake Faith

And why do you, by your traditions, violate the direct commandments of God? For instance, God says, "Honor your father and mother," and "Anyone who speaks disrespectfully of father or mother must be put to death." But you say it is all right for people to say to their parents, "Sorry, I can't help you. For I have vowed to give to God what I would have given to you." In this way, you say they don't need to honor their parents. And so you cancel the word of God for the sake of your own tradition.

Matthew 15:3–6 NLT

Jesus has just been challenged by some religious leaders whose goal is to make him look bad by accusing him of ignoring their laws and traditions. They're slamming him for not going through a somewhat ridiculous and very tedious ceremonial hand-washing exercise before eating. But Jesus tosses the question right back at them. His purpose is to point out their hypocrisy and selfishness because he knows how they manipulate religious laws for their own benefit. He is aware of how these supposed religious leaders get rich at the expense of the very people they are supposed to be serving.

To further drive his point home, Jesus quotes from one of their own prophets, Isaiah, by saying, "These people honor me with their lips, but their hearts are far from me. Their worship is a farce, for they teach man-made ideas as commands from God" (vv. 8–9 NLT).

It seems that nothing aggravated Jesus more than religious hypocrisy. In fact, the only times Jesus showed real anger was in regard to religious fakers. Who could blame him? What is worse than someone pretending to be godly so they can take advantage of others? It's like they think they can use God for their own benefit, whether it's a TV evangelist who extorts money from a poor, guilt-ridden viewer, or a teenage girl who fakes her Christian faith in order to get the attention of a cool Christian guy. It all stinks.

Jesus wants you to avoid being a fake by keeping your faith authentic and honest—straight from the heart. Really, why would you settle for anything less?

My Prayer

Dear God,
Help me to keep my faith real, even if it means admitting my faults to others. Teach me to guard my heart against hypocrisy.
Amen.

Stone
for the Journey

I will keep my faith real.

Final Word

Give me understanding, that I may observe Your law and keep it with all my heart.

Psalm 119:34 NASB

Weight of Words

Words from the Rock

Listen . . . and try to understand. It's not what goes into your mouth that defiles you; you are defiled by the words that come out of your mouth.

Matthew 15:10–11 NLT

Jesus makes a bold statement here. On the surface he seems to be addressing the religious leaders' compulsive obsession about ceremonial hand washing before eating, but his true meaning is much deeper. Remember how the hypocritical religious leaders had criticized Jesus and his disciples, saying they were defiled and dirty because they had eaten their lunch with "unclean" hands? Jesus tells these men that even if they eat "dirty" food, it wouldn't hurt them—not like it would hurt them if they speak dirty words.

And wasn't this what the Pharisees were doing? Those phonies acted like they were so clean and pure—better than everyone else. But it was only on the surface. Underneath their fancy robes and "good" manners, and beneath their disguise of godliness, they were selfish and mean and hypocritical. While pretending to serve God, they were actually conniving to trip up God's own Son and the world's

Savior. This was made obvious by the words that spilled from their mouths.

That was Jesus's point. It's not what goes *into* our mouths that messes us up; it's what comes *out* of them. Our words reflect what's inside of us. Even if we try to sugarcoat them to hide something corrupt, our true feelings can be revealed through a single slip of the tongue. It's better to clean up what's inside of us than to act like everything's cool on the exterior. To do that, we need God's help.

My Prayer

Dear God,
I realize I need your help to cleanse my heart.
Please do your work in me so my words will
show that I really do belong to you.
Amen.

Final Word

Stone
for the Journey

My words represent what God is doing inside me.

Don't just pretend to love others. Really love them. Hate what is wrong. Hold tightly to what is good.

Romans 12:9 NLT

Religious Traps

Words from the Rock

> *Every plant not planted by my heavenly Father*
> *will be uprooted, so ignore [the Pharisees]. They*
> *are blind guides leading the blind, and if one blind*
> *person guides another, they will both fall into a*
> *ditch.*
>
> Matthew 15:13–14 NLT

*J*esus is describing religious hypocrites again, plainly stating that despite the Pharisees' "godly" claims, they do not truly represent God. Jesus knew that God would eventually take away their so-called authority by uprooting them. In the meantime, he warned his followers to ignore leaders like them. He understood that their form of religion was to bind people with ridiculous legalistic restrictions, to the point where they became too distracted to see God or to recognize his Son.

It's like those leaders were religious traps. They were set on ensnaring people and essentially preventing them from hearing or understanding the real truth—Jesus. Fortunately, Jesus was able to cut through their deceptive ways again and again. He did this openly and publicly so that his followers would remember these incidents when Jesus was no longer physically living among them.

Did you know there are still religious traps today? These traps come in many disguises, but most of them are rooted in legalism, not God. Legalism happens when we create or follow man-made rules in order to make ourselves "acceptable" to God. When we believe that it's our own actions that earn our way to God, we have fallen into a religious trap. Time and again Jesus says we come to God through him—via his grace, his forgiveness, his love. Thankfully, that's not something we can manufacture on our own.

My Prayer

Dear God,
Help me to remember that the only way to you is through your Son. Don't let me fall into any religious traps—whether of my own making or someone else's.
Amen.

Stone
for the Journey

I will not be led astray by legalism.

Final Word

We say with confidence, "The Lord is my helper; I will not be afraid. What can man do to me?"

Hebrews 13:6 NIV

19

Real Sign

Words from the Rock

If the sky is red in the evening, you say the weather will be good. But if the sky is red and gloomy in the morning, you say it is going to rain. You can tell what the weather will be like by looking at the sky. But you don't understand what is happening now. You want a sign because you are evil and won't believe! But the only sign you will be given is what happened to Jonah.

Matthew 16:2–4 CEV

Those religious leaders are trying to trip up Jesus again. Is it just that they have nothing better to do, or are they simply afraid that he's going to ruin their influence on the people? Whatever the case, they have just demanded that Jesus show them a "sign from heaven" to prove he was really sent from God. Naturally, Jesus declines their invitation, making it clear that it is God who calls the shots, not them. Then he points out that they are better at predicting the weather than they are at understanding God.

The arrogance of these supposed leaders is actually pretty mind-blowing. Do they honestly think they can force Jesus to send them a sign from heaven while they clearly refuse to accept that he is who he says he is? Isn't that kind of like challenging Michael Jordan to prove he's Michael Jordan by insisting he engage in a game of one-on-one with you?

Not only does Jesus deny these jokers' request, but he tells them that the only sign they'll get is "what happened to Jonah." And Jonah was swallowed by a whale after he refused to listen to God. Hint hint.

So how does this apply to you and your life today? Is it possible that Jesus doesn't want your faith to be the result of some supernatural sign sent down from heaven? Jesus wants you to believe in him because you've personally experienced his love and forgiveness. He wants you to be so rooted in him and to make him so much a part of your life that your faith is sort of organic—it has simply grown out of your relationship with him, almost like you can't help it. You are beginning to look and act like him—and that's a real sign from heaven!

My Prayer

Dear God,
I don't need you to send down flashy signs from heaven to prove yourself to me. Help me to remember the best sign you can give me is the quiet work you do inside my heart.
Amen.

Stone
for the Journey

Jesus in me
is the best
sign of God's
existence.

Final Word

Finishing is better than starting! Patience is better than pride!

Ecclesiastes 7:8 TLB

20

Who Is He?

Words from the Rock

Simon, son of Jonah, you are blessed! You didn't discover this on your own. It was shown to you by my Father in heaven. So I will call you Peter, which means "a rock." On this rock I will build my church, and death itself will not have any power over it. I will give you the keys to the kingdom of heaven, and God in heaven will allow whatever you allow on earth. But he will not allow anything that you don't allow.

Matthew 16:17–19 CEV

This is quite a promise that Jesus has just given to Simon Peter. It's in response to a conversation Jesus just had with his disciples. He asked them what people were saying about him, and they answered that some people thought he was John the Baptist, others thought he was one of the old prophets such as Elijah or Jeremiah. Then Jesus asked his disciples what they thought: "What about you? . . . Who do you say I am?" (Matt. 16:15 NIV).

It was Peter's answer that blew Jesus away: "You are the Christ, the Son of the living God" (v. 16 NIV). And that's when Jesus gives

Peter that amazing blessing. He also points out that Peter's answer is correct only because God had revealed it to him. Jesus knows that because God had revealed these things, Peter is truly the best choice to lead what would soon become the first church.

This must have been a happy day for Peter. His faith truly did seem rock solid. For Jesus to commend him like that . . . well, Peter must have been just about bursting with pride. Yet the day would come when Peter would deny Jesus—not just once but three times. And still Jesus would build his church on Peter.

Jesus wants all his followers to know who he is. If he came to you today and asked you, "Who am I?" how would you answer? Do you understand that your answer matters? Would you call him your friend or just a casual acquaintance? Would you say he's a nice guy or the Son of God? Would you describe him as your Lord and Savior or just a godly man who once walked the earth? Who is he to you?

My Prayer

Dear God,
Please show me who you are in my life. Son of God, Lord, Savior, reveal to me who you are and help me to proclaim it.
Amen.

Stone
for the Journey

When I know who Jesus is, I will know who I am.

Final Word

We know that Jesus Christ the Son of God has come and has shown us the true God. And because of Jesus, we now belong to the true God who gives eternal life.

1 John 5:20 CEV

Kingdom Keys

> *And that's not all. You will have complete and free access to God's kingdom, keys to open any and every door: no more barriers between heaven and earth, earth and heaven. A yes on earth is yes in heaven. A no on earth is no in heaven.*
>
> Matthew 16:19 Message

It's an awesome feeling when your parents hand you the keys to the car for the first time. But what Jesus gives to Peter (after hearing Peter's correct answer) is far better. Jesus is handing over the keys to God's kingdom, promising Peter that he can open all doors and that there will be nothing to separate him from heaven. His words on earth will have the same weight in heaven. What a deal! And all this just because Peter knows who Jesus is—because he understands that Jesus is God's Son, the one who has come to save the world. Peter's reward is the keys to the kingdom.

Guess what? The same reward is offered to anyone who acknowledges Jesus in the same way Peter did. We all have equal access to the kingdom keys, but some people get confused. They think if they have the keys to the kingdom, it'll be like having a magic wand that they can wave, and whatever they want will be theirs. Wrong.

The real key is *knowing* Jesus—and when we truly know Jesus, all we want to do is what he wants us to do. As a result, our "yes" on earth really does become a "yes" in heaven. When we ask for something, we receive it—because our goal is to do things according to God's perfect will, not our own.

Naturally, this doesn't happen overnight. It's a day-by-day, faith-walking process that is carried out one step at a time.

My Prayer

Dear God,
Help me to really know you so I can have access to your kingdom keys and live my life within your perfect will.
Amen.

Stone
for the Journey

The more I know God, the more I know his will.

Final Word

If any of you lacks wisdom, he should ask God, who gives generously to all without finding fault, and it will be given to him.

James 1:5 NIV

Followers

> *If anyone would come after me, he must deny himself and take up his cross and follow me.*
>
> Matthew 16:24 NIV

*J*esus has just been talking to his disciples about his impending death, but they're in total shock and disbelief. Even Peter (remember, the faithful rock?) doubts Jesus's sensibilities here, and Jesus actually reprimands him for it.

Clearly, the context of this Scripture is death. Jesus is talking about dying literally. His words about taking up his cross are in direct reference to the cross he will be nailed to, the cross he will die on. His disciples are stunned. Furthermore, they wonder if Jesus is asking them to die alongside him. Maybe so. Time will tell.

This is not an easy message for anyone to hear, and not something to be taken lightly. But what does it mean for you? What Jesus implies in this verse is that if you truly want to follow him and honestly want to be his disciple, you must be willing to put your own plans to death. To be completely faithful to Jesus, you have to nail your own hopes and expectations to the cross. You do this in exchange for the guidance and direction he will give you, and then you are ready to be led.

It's kind of like getting out of the driver's seat and letting Jesus get in. So even if it looks like you're about to get in a big wreck, you sit there on the passenger side and trust Jesus's ability to drive. Even if you're nervous, you don't try to grab the steering wheel away from him. Although he might take a different road than you would have, or drive a little faster or a whole lot slower than you'd like, you know that he will get you to where you need to go. Once you settle in and really trust him, you will actually enjoy the trip, and you will be extremely thankful when you arrive at a place that exceeds all your original hopes, dreams, and expectations!

My Prayer

Dear God,
Help me to trust you so implicitly that I allow you to lead in every aspect of my life. Teach me to follow you wherever you want to lead.
Amen.

Stone
for the Journey

Only as I set aside my will can I find God's.

Final Word

If you love me, you will do what I have said, and my Father will love you. I will also love you and show you what I am like.

John 14:21 CEV

23

Lost and Found

Words from the Rock

For whoever wants to save his life will lose it, but whoever loses his life for me will find it.

Matthew 16:25 NIV

*L*ife, death, commitment—these are all pretty heavy topics. And Jesus doesn't sugarcoat his message one bit. He's telling his disciples that they're entering into an all-or-nothing sort of agreement. He's making a very somber prediction—that they will lose their lives for him someday. In fact, after Jesus's death and resurrection, ten of his disciples (and many other followers) will eventually be put to death for following him. Yet they will not waver in their faith. Not one of them will regret their commitment to him or the pain and suffering as a result of it.

But what do these words mean for you personally? Is Jesus literally asking you to be killed for believing in him? Probably not, since that's not happening much in the United States these days (although Christians are put to death for their faith in some countries). Even so, these words should pack a pretty stiff punch.

Jesus is saying that if you love your life more than you love him—if you cling to your own dreams more tightly than you cling to him—your life and your dreams will slip right through your fingers, and you will lose everything completely.

On the other hand, if you give up your life for Jesus (remember the steering wheel image?), if you surrender all control to him, he will give you back a life that's far beyond anything you could ever hope for. But you have to let go first. You have to trust him with everything. You have to believe that only God knows what you truly need—only Jesus in the driver's seat will get you where you really need to go.

My Prayer

Dear God,
I really don't want to lose my life. Show me how to let go, and help me to trust you completely. Thank you for getting me to where I need to go. Amen.

Stone
for the Journey

When I lose my life for God, I will find it.

Final Word

Because he has loved Me, therefore I will deliver him; I will set him securely on high, because he has known My name.

Psalm 91:14 NASB

How Much?

> *What will you gain, if you own the whole world*
> *but destroy yourself? What would you give to get*
> *back your soul?*
>
> Matthew 16:26 CEV

*S*ome people will do anything to get rich. Some will even lie, cheat, and steal to get what they want. Others will simply work incredibly hard—shoving all else aside to make "success" their number one goal. Now there's nothing wrong with hard work or earning an honest living, but that's not Jesus's point in this particular verse.

Jesus is giving us a warning. He understands how we think and what motivates us. He's aware of common human character flaws such as greed, pride, and selfishness. He knows that we are all subject to these weaknesses. He also knows that the *love* of money and material things will ultimately lead to our destruction. He comprehends the way our hearts work and knows that if we value anything above God, it will be our undoing.

It's not easy living in a materialistic world where merchandise and fads are constantly thrust in our faces, where credit cards are pressed into the hands of teenagers, and where millions of dollars are spent on marketing items that promise happiness. But Jesus is saying not to fall for those lies. Don't be caught up in "having it all." Don't be trapped into thinking that more is better, because the end result is always the same—you lose. People who spend all their time and energy accumulating this world's riches will end up spiritually bankrupt. And by the time they figure it out, it will be too late. Jesus doesn't want you to be one of them.

My Prayer

Dear God,
Please help me to remember that material things will not bring me real or lasting happiness. Help me to value you above all else and to keep you first in my life.
Amen.

Stone
for the Journey

I will not trade my soul for earthly riches.

Final Word

The love of money causes all kinds of trouble. Some people want money so much that they have given up their faith and caused themselves a lot of pain.

1 Timothy 6:10 CEV

Real Hunger

Words from the Rock

Truly, truly, I say to you, you seek Me, not because you saw signs, but because you ate of the loaves and were filled. Do not work for the food which perishes, but for the food which endures to eternal life, which the Son of Man will give to you, for on Him the Father, God, has set His seal.

John 6:26–27 NASB

Jesus knows that his time on earth is limited, yet he has this huge message to get across. Unfortunately, human minds have difficulty grasping spiritual meanings. Not to mention they are easily distracted by things as ordinary as hunger or boredom. Jesus's popularity is on the rise, but it may have more to do with people looking for food and entertainment than the realization that they are spiritually starving.

Yet Jesus understands people. Plus he is aware that times are hard, and he knows how his followers relate and respond to basic necessities like food and drink. So he uses these rather ordinary images to connect to the people. First Jesus candidly tells them that they're seeking him for food. He calls a spade a spade. Then he points out that it's not spiritual food they're looking for either. They simply want something to fill their bellies—perhaps some more of that delicious bread and fish with which he fed the thousands.

Jesus tells the people that he has another kind of nourishment to offer them—a kind of food that will feed their souls and change their lives, a kind of food that's been sent from his Father. It's the same thing he offers to you—a piece of himself. He wants you to be as hungry for him as you are for your favorite food. In fact, he wants you to be even hungrier for him. Food is here and gone just like that, and then you get hungry again. But what Jesus offers will satisfy that deep inner longing in a way that a pizza simply can't.

My Prayer

Dear God,
I want to be hungry for you. Help me to see that my soul needs your nourishment even more than my stomach needs food.
Amen.

Final Word

The eyes of the LORD range throughout the earth to strengthen those whose hearts are fully committed to him.

2 Chronicles 16:9 NIV

Stone
for the Journey

My spiritual hunger can only be satisfied by God.

Job Description

Words from the Rock

This is the only work God wants from you: Believe in the one he has sent.

John 6:29 NLT

*W*e live in a culture where jobs and work are taken fairly seriously. Most high schools put a lot of emphasis on planning for college, focusing on career options, offering work-study programs or internships, and generally preparing you for life as a responsible, self-supporting adult. That's all well and good, and your parents probably encourage these same ideals—since they don't want to support you forever—but Jesus plainly says that the only work God has for you is to believe in him.

So does that mean you won't need to get a job? Probably not. What it does mean is that there is nothing more important for you to invest your time and energy in than the maintenance of your faith. Your most important work is to believe in the one God has sent.

In other words, God wants you to take your faith even more seriously than you would a career. That means you must work at it. Some of the ways you can do that are by reading and studying God's Word, praying regularly, attending some form of fellowship, and sharing God's Good News with others. But mostly you need to work on the condition of your heart by keeping it right with God. That's your job—yours alone—and God says it's the most important thing you can do. And here's some more good news: the more diligently you work on maintaining your faith, the more God will direct you in other things like finding the perfect career. So really, it's a win-win situation.

My Prayer

Dear God,
Help me to remember that you want me to work at believing in you. Show me new ways to do this—and help me not to be a slacker.
Amen.

Stone
for the Journey

My most important job is to believe in God.

Final Word

Trust in the LORD with all your heart and lean not on your own understanding; in all your ways acknowledge him, and he will make your paths straight.

Proverbs 3:5–6 NIV

Soul Food

> *I am the bread that gives life. Whoever comes to me will never be hungry again. Whoever believes in me will never be thirsty.*
>
> John 6:35 NLT

This is a very bold statement, and one that many of Jesus's listeners could not quite wrap their heads around. Was Jesus suggesting that they were supposed to turn cannibal and actually eat him? Seriously, some people asked this very question. Yet this is only the beginning of what will be a long string of food metaphors in which Jesus doesn't simply compare himself to food; he actually says he is food.

Of course, you probably know by now (at least in your head) that Jesus is talking about spiritual food. The problem is that he's trying to get this message across to an audience who isn't very good at listening with spiritual ears. To them, food is food, drink is drink. They're confused.

Maybe you are too. Can you grasp the reality that Jesus wants you to be so connected to him that it's almost as if you had physically consumed him? He wants to be such an integral part of your life that it's as if he's asking you to take a great big bite of him and hold that within you. Maybe that creeps you out. If that's the case, it's because you're hearing his words with your physical ears instead of your spiritual ones.

Jesus wants to pour himself into you so much that you won't feel spiritually empty or famished. He wants to nurture that deep hunger inside of you until you're full. He wants to satisfy you with himself, his love, his forgiveness, his mercy, his joy, his grace—so many things he wants to fill you up with. But until you recognize that you're spiritually starving without him, he can't do it. He doesn't force himself on anyone.

My Prayer

Dear God,
I know that I'm spiritually hungry, but sometimes I forget to come to you. Please fill my empty spaces with all you have for me. Satisfy my longing with your presence.
Amen.

Stone
for the Journey

Only God can fill the emptiness inside of me.

Final Word

As the deer pants for water, so I long for you, O God. I thirst for God, the living God. Where can I find him to come and stand before him?

Psalm 42:1–2 TLB

28

No Rejection

> *Those the Father has given me will come to me,*
> *and I will never reject them. For I have come down*
> *from heaven to do the will of God who sent me,*
> *not to do my own will. And this is the will of God,*
> *that I should not lose even one of all those he has*
> *given me, but that I should raise them up at the*
> *last day.*
>
> John 6:37–39 NLT

Everyone gets rejected by someone sometime. If it hasn't happened to you yet, just wait, it will. It's just the way life goes. But Jesus promises that he will *never* reject you. That's a promise you can count on. Jesus also wants his listeners to understand that not only will he never reject them, but that he has come to do God's will as well. He directly connects himself to God, but at the same time he makes it perfectly clear that God is the one calling the shots, not Jesus.

Jesus knows these people have a basic, although somewhat flawed, understanding of God. He hopes that their respect for and belief in

God will somehow translate into how they relate to him as God's ambassador. Jesus also knows (thanks to those hypocritical Pharisees and other religious leaders) that the people he's addressing have a serious fear of God's rejection. Day in and day out it hangs over their heads like a black cloud—that all-consuming worry that if they don't live their lives "perfectly" (according to a bunch of impossibly crazy laws), God will reject them. What a heavy load to carry.

Somehow Jesus must convince them (and us) that not only will he never reject anyone, but he will also make a way for everyone to be reunited with God—permanently. That's an even greater promise—no rejection and a never-ending connection. Of course, at this point Jesus isn't finished with his work on earth. Consequently, his listeners still feel confused. But just hearing the sweet promise that Jesus would never reject them must have been a huge comfort. It's a promise you can cling to as well.

My Prayer

Dear God,
Thank you for accepting me just as I am. Thank you that you will never reject me. Please help me to never reject you either!
Amen.

Stone
for the Journey

God will never reject me.

Final Word

What can we ever say to such wonderful things as these? If God is on our side, who can ever be against us?

Romans 8:31 TLB

29

Big Promise

> The Father is the One who sent me. No one can
> come to me unless the Father draws him to me,
> and I will raise that person up on the last day. . . .
> No one has seen the Father except the One who is
> from God; only he has seen the Father. I tell you
> the truth, whoever believes has eternal life.
>
> John 6:44, 46–47 NCV

Jesus is drawing a tight connection between himself and God. It's imperative that people get this. If they don't understand that God is his Father and that Jesus and God are one, the plan for salvation will all unravel. Jesus knows this is a tough concept for people. They have questions and doubts. How can an earthly man also be God's Son? How is it possible that this Jesus dude, who looks normal and has no wings, has really come from heaven? It just does not compute. Not yet anyway.

They also question how Jesus is able to make such huge promises. How is he able to guarantee that *he* can give them eternal life? As much as they may want to believe this is possible, it's a struggle.

Again, it's because Jesus's work on earth isn't done yet. In time it will begin to make more sense—missing pieces of the puzzle will appear and the full picture will be revealed.

Fortunately, we have those pieces now. We know the full story. Yet sometimes we're like Jesus's listeners who were still in the dark. We struggle with our own doubts and questions. Maybe we tell ourselves that it sounds too good to be true. Or we question how it's possible that Jesus can really make such an amazing offer. But Jesus just keeps it simple. He clearly states that if we believe in him, we will have eternal life. He's taken care of everything for us. Except for one thing—we have to choose to believe in him. That's up to us.

My Prayer

Dear God,
I do believe in you. I believe you sent Jesus to show me the way to you. I believe that you have already given me eternal life. Help my faith to grow stronger.
Amen.

> ### Stone
> *for the Journey*
>
> **My belief in Jesus is my ticket to eternity.**

Final Word

Anyone who believes in God's Son has eternal life. Anyone who doesn't obey the Son will never experience eternal life but remains under God's angry judgment.

John 3:36 NLT

30

Living Bread

Words from the Rock

I am the bread of life. . . . I am the living bread that came down from heaven. If anyone eats of this bread, he will live forever. This bread is my flesh, which I will give for the life of the world.

John 6:48, 51 NIV

Jesus doesn't simply compare himself to food—he plainly states that he *is* food. He is the Bread of Life. He has been sent from heaven. Anyone who eats of him will live forever.

These are hard words for his listeners to swallow. Again their minds leap to things like cannibalism, and they recall some of the strange heathen religions where people do creepy things like sacrificing humans. Surely that's not what Jesus is saying! Or is it?

Again Jesus puts emphasis on the fact that he came from heaven. He's not earthly bread. He's not trying to introduce a new cannibal religion. He just wants his listeners to open their spiritual ears and really hear what he means. He wants them to know that he longs to be as closely connected to them as that chunk of barley bread and olive oil they consumed for lunch, which gave them energy and nourishment. Jesus wants to be as immersed into their beings as the red wine with which they washed down the bread is immersed into their bloodstream. He doesn't want this to happen in the physical sense—you get that by now—but in the spiritual sense.

Jesus loves us so much that he wants to be a vital part of our lives. He wants to be tightly connected, to be united, to be one with us. He wants to flow through our lives, and he wants us to welcome his presence in the same way our bodies welcome wholesome food.

My Prayer

Dear God,
I invite you to fill me with all the goodness you have for me. Help me to ingest you into my being until I am full.
Amen.

> # Stone
> *for the Journey*
>
> **Jesus is the Bread that gives me life.**

Final Word

He satisfies the thirsty and fills up the hungry.
Psalm 107:9 NCV

31

Life Blood

Words from the Rock

I tell you the truth, unless you eat the flesh of the Son of Man and drink his blood, you cannot have eternal life within you. . . . For my flesh is true food, and my blood is true drink. Anyone who eats my flesh and drinks my blood remains in me, and I in him.

John 6:53, 55–56 NLT

Imagine the horrified gasps that might have been heard when Jesus made this startling statement. Again, was he really telling them to eat his flesh and drink his blood? Or maybe they didn't hear him right. Some listeners might have been so disgusted that they turned and hurried away. Others might have been so caught up in the sensation that they wanted more—similar to the way drivers slow down to gape at a nasty traffic accident. The reactions probably varied, but you can be sure Jesus got everyone's attention when he spoke these words.

It was one thing for Jesus to call himself the Bread of Life and invite them to eat that bread. Perhaps they were even starting to understand this on some level. Now suddenly he's telling them to eat his flesh and drink his blood. How can this be? What does it really mean?

Blood is a symbol of both life and death. And Jesus offers both life and death to everyone. He is inviting us to participate in his life by first participating in his death. He knows that his physical blood will soon be shed and that his earthly life will come to an end. He also knows that it's only through his death that the entire human race will finally be reunited with God the Father, and it's only through the spilling of his blood that he can offer them real life, eternal life.

Of course, his listeners can't grasp this. Even his loyal disciples don't get it. They don't want Jesus to die. And they certainly don't want to drink his blood. They're just as confused as anyone. Maybe you feel confused too. Maybe it's overwhelming to think about things like drinking Jesus's blood. But remember, Jesus is speaking in spiritual terms. He is simply offering himself and his death as your ticket to eternal life. Blood equals life. But again, in order to receive it, you must be willing to accept it.

My Prayer

Dear God,
Thank you for this amazing gift of life. I know that the cost was Jesus's death and his blood, and I am ready to embrace that. Thank you! Amen.

Stone
for the Journey

Jesus's blood equals eternal life for me.

Final Word

All mankind scratches for its daily bread, but your heavenly Father knows your needs.

Luke 12:30 TLB

Life Bread

Words from the Rock

I live because of the living Father who sent me; in the same way, anyone who feeds on me will live because of me. I am the true bread that came down from heaven. Anyone who eats this bread will not die as your ancestors did (even though they ate the manna) but will live forever.

John 6:57–58 NLT

Do you think Jesus repeated himself simply because he liked the sound of his own voice? No, of course not. It was only because he knew that his listeners weren't getting it. He had to make this whole thing as clear as possible, even if that meant pounding it into them. He was offering the words of life, and they needed to get a hold on them.

He drives home his point even more by reminding his listeners of their ancestors, because he knows that everyone there has heard the old story—how Moses led the children of Israel out of captivity in Egypt, how they got hungry out in the wilderness, and how

God rained down bread from heaven to feed them. It was a happy, miraculous story that they'd heard repeated since childhood.

Then Jesus reminds them that those same ancestors, the ones who enjoyed that heavenly bread, still died in the end. Although the bread filled their bellies for a while, it didn't give them eternal life. Jesus wants you to understand that God created a deep-down hunger inside of you. If you try to fill that hunger with pizzas, cheeseburgers, or fries (which might add to your waistline), you'll still be spiritually starving. Until you get that Jesus is the only one who can satisfy that hunger, you'll try to fill the void with something else.

Jesus is the Bread of Heaven. When he's inside you, you're satisfied and full, and you have eternal life. Why would you want to settle for less?

My Prayer

Dear God,
I realize that I'm spiritually hungry. I want Jesus, the Bread of Life, to fill that emptiness inside of me.
Amen.

Stone
for the Journey

Jesus satisfies my deepest hunger.

Final Word

My God will meet all your needs according to his glorious riches in Christ Jesus.

Philippians 4:19 NIV

33

Wrong Expectations

Words from the Rock

Does this throw you completely? What would happen if you saw the Son of Man ascending to where he came from? The Spirit can make life. Sheer muscle and will-power don't make anything happen. Every word I've spoken to you is a Spirit-word, and so it is life-making. . . . This is why I told you earlier that no one is capable of coming to me on his own. You get to me only as a gift from the Father.

John 6:61–63, 65 Message

Jesus knows his words have really stretched his audience. He knows they're confused and doubtful and possibly on the verge of just giving up. Perhaps they wonder why he doesn't just tell them some more of those "nice" stories or do some healing miracles. Or maybe all his talk about bread has gotten their stomachs growling, and they're wishing he'd just pull out some loaves and fishes and feed everyone.

Instead he's pulling out the big guns. He's laying it on the line, spelling it out that he really is the Son of Man and that he's been sent from his Father. Everything he's telling them is spiritual, and he gives them words of life. Maybe you wonder why it's so hard for them to get it. Why does he have to keep pounding it into them?

For one thing, it's not yet time for them to fully grasp who he is or exactly why he came. Jesus is aware of this. He knows he's doing the groundwork. But the other reason, perhaps the bigger reason, is that the way God's will is going to play out is not what these people expect. This is not the way they thought God would work. Thanks to some of their faulty leaders and wrong assumptions, they just never expected God to send them salvation and life in this way. Now maybe if Jesus was clothed in shining white garments trimmed in gold, and perhaps if he rode in on a huge white horse, shooting fire from his fingertips . . . well, that might have been more like it.

But that's not how God is working. His plan is bigger and better and far beyond anything their human minds could imagine or dream. Yet they find it hard to budge from their old, worn-out, and wrong expectations. They had learned long ago to put God in a box, and it's very difficult for them to let him out. Yet Jesus is getting ready to break that box wide open.

My Prayer

Dear God,
Help me never to put you in a box. Remind me of how big you are and how you work in my life in some unexpected but amazing ways.
Amen.

Stone
for the Journey

My God is full of surprises.

Final Word

Because of Christ and our faith in him, we can now come boldly and confidently into God's presence.

Ephesians 3:12 NLT

34

Recognize Truth

Words from the Rock

The things I teach are not my own, but they come from him who sent me. If people choose to do what God wants, they will know that my teaching comes from God and not from me. Those who teach their own ideas are trying to get honor for themselves. But those who try to bring honor to the one who sent them speak the truth, and there is nothing false in them.

John 7:16–18 NCV

Jesus has just been teaching in the temple, and suddenly he's being questioned and challenged. While it's perfectly acceptable for "learned" men to teach casually in the temple, the Jews questioning Jesus don't believe he's had sufficient education. Perhaps they're threatened by him, or maybe his words have made them uncomfortable. And don't forget that these people are still stuck in their own wrong expectations. Their comfort zone is to keep God safely in a box.

Again Jesus cuts to the chase. He tells the Jews in no uncertain terms that he's not teaching his own ideas or personal opinions (unlike the Pharisees); he is simply teaching God's truth. He also tells them that if they were truly connected to God, they would know that Jesus really is God's spokesman (in fact, God's own Son). But these men are still in the dark. They are still caught up in their own misinformed beliefs. Sure, they might be hoping for the coming of the Christ (the Messiah), but they are certain that Jesus could not be the real deal.

This is, in fact, the question that every single person must face in their own lifetime—is Jesus really the Son of God, and if he is, what does that mean to them personally? When we remain caught up in our own false beliefs and wrong expectations, and when we refuse to accept that Jesus was sent from God, we are essentially rejecting God's love and forgiveness, since that's what Jesus came to earth to give us. But when we believe that Jesus is sent from God, when we embrace his truth and receive his love and forgiveness, then we are connected to God, not only here on earth but for eternity.

My Prayer

Dear God,
Please teach me to separate fact from fiction.
Show me how to know the difference between what is your truth and what isn't.
Amen.

Stone
for the Journey

God's truth is unchanging.

Final Word

> As for God, His way is perfect; the word of the LORD is proven; He is a shield to all who trust in Him.
>
> Psalm 18:30 NKJV

35

Learn to Discern

Words from the Rock

I did one miraculous thing a few months ago, and you're still standing around getting all upset, wondering what I'm up to. . . . Don't be nitpickers; use your head—and heart!—to discern what is right, to test what is authentically right.

John 7:21, 24 Message

Imagine that you're a doctor and you hear about a far-off island where all the people suffer from some horrible, deadly disease. Now imagine that you have the only cure, a vaccine you invented, and you decide to get it to them. It's going to cost you—you must sell your home and fancy car to afford enough of the vaccine, but you do it anyway. Then you travel to the island, and although the people are sick and dying, they refuse to believe that you're really a doctor or that your vaccination will save their lives. How frustrating!

In a small way, that might have been how Jesus felt. We probably have no idea how frustrated he must have been at times. He knew who he was, he knew who had sent him, he knew he had the words of life . . . and yet sometimes it seemed as if no one was getting it. Or else they were getting distracted and arguing over silly things—kind of just muddying up the waters.

Sometimes we do the exact same thing. We turn into religious nitpickers and get into ridiculous arguments over whether the Bible said this or that. Instead of remembering that the main message of the Bible is to love one another, we use the Bible to beat each other up. Jesus is saying to use our heads *and our hearts* so we can understand what's right (and what's wrong). In other words, he's saying we need to develop discernment—we need to be able to recognize when something is true or not, when something is good or not. But to learn how to do that, we need to go to him, because he's the one who gives discernment.

My Prayer

Dear God,
Help me to be discerning. Teach me to use both my heart and my head to think, and help me to avoid silly arguments.
Amen.

Stone
for the Journey

God can teach me to use my head and my heart.

Final Word

> *Do not conform any longer to the pattern of this world, but be transformed by the renewing of your mind. Then you will be able to test and approve what God's will is—his good, pleasing and perfect will.*

> Romans 12:2 NIV

36

The Connector

Words from the Rock

Yes, you know me, and you know where I am from. But I have not come by my own authority. I was sent by the One who is true, whom you don't know. But I know him, because I am from him, and he sent me.

John 7:28–29 NCV

Jesus has just been teaching in the temple, and suddenly it seems that the light is starting to click on in some people's minds. They actually begin to talk among themselves, speculating about whether or not Jesus really might be the Messiah. This is a real milestone for Jesus's ministry. They're starting to get it!

So he directs this statement to them. He tells them they are absolutely right, that they have recognized him, and that their suspicions about where he's come from (God) are on target. His words probably catch them by surprise since they'd been whispering among themselves. It would seem that he has their full attention. And that's when he points out that they don't really know God.

Although Jesus is simply being honest and direct, it probably feels like a slap in the face to these religious men. Especially since they're in the temple at the time, putting on a pretense of godliness. So these men, now angered and offended, attempt to have Jesus arrested. It's not time for that yet, so despite their efforts, Jesus just slips away.

But his point has been made. Jesus knows God because he is from God, and God is the one who sent him. Once again it's all about connection—Jesus is connected to God, and he wants to be the one to connect you to God. He knows that without that connection, you'll easily be misled and confused, and life will be empty and meaningless.

My Prayer

Dear God,
I do want to be connected to you. Thank you for all that you've done to be connected to me. Help me to remain connected always.
Amen.

Stone
for the Journey

I know God,
and he
knows me.

Final Word

> *Therefore everyone who hears these words of mine and puts them into practice is like a wise man who built his house on the rock.*

Matthew 7:24 NIV

37

Mountain Movers

Words from the Rock

What a generation! No sense of God! No focus to your lives! How many times do I have to go over these things? How much longer do I have to put up with this? . . . You're not yet taking God seriously. . . . The simple truth is that if you had a mere kernel of faith, a poppy seed, say, you would tell this mountain, "Move!" and it would move. There is nothing you wouldn't be able to tackle.

Matthew 17:17, 20 Message

Can't you just hear the frustration in Jesus's words? It's like he's standing there with his arms outstretched and holding out all the answers for them, yet the people won't take them. It's like their minds are stuck and they can't really believe him. They hesitate and balk and doubt and question him. They never quite get to that place where they really grasp what he's trying to give them. It must have been a challenge for him to remain patient.

In this portion of Scripture, Jesus's disciples have just asked him to help them heal an epileptic boy. He has made it clear that they already have what it takes to do these miraculous healings themselves because of their connection with him. But they hold up their hands helplessly and plead with him because it's not working. So Jesus steps in once again and heals the boy. Then he uses this opportunity to remind them that it takes only a tiny bit of faith on their part—a tiny mustard seed is all that's needed to do great things. If they took God seriously, they could do anything with his help.

The cool thing is that before long (after Jesus's death and resurrection), these same disciples are doing all kinds of amazing miracles. Things turn out just as Jesus said. Their seed-sized faith grows into something huge and powerful, something even greater than moving a mountain—their faith and works change the history of the entire world.

My Prayer

Dear God,
Sometimes my faith seems smaller than a mustard seed. Please remind me that you can do anything, and that all I need to do is believe in you and my faith will grow.
Amen.

> **Stone**
> *for the Journey*
>
> **I will plant my seed-sized faith in God.**

Final Word

> *Don't fall for that nonsense. This is your Father you are dealing with, and he knows better than you what you need.*
>
> Matthew 6:8 Message

38

Three-Part Plan

The Son of Man is going to be betrayed into the hands of men. They will kill him, and on the third day he will be raised to life.

Matthew 17:22–23 NIV

Although Jesus predicts his death and resurrection several times, it almost seems that his disciples aren't paying attention—or maybe they don't really believe it will happen. Especially when you see how rattled they become when Jesus is arrested and crucified—it's like they're blindsided. Or maybe they're simply in deep denial because they love him so much and don't want him to leave. Whatever the case, Jesus doesn't keep his impending death a secret. He lays it out there for his disciples to see.

To be fair, it would be pretty shocking to have a dear friend tell you that (1) he's going to be betrayed, (2) he's going to be killed, and (3) after three days he'll come back from the dead. That's a lot to wrap your head around.

You have to appreciate that Jesus doesn't keep this plan to himself. It's not like he's trying to surprise anyone (although the whole world would eventually be astounded). As always, Jesus is up-front with his disciples. He lays his cards on the table by telling them exactly what's coming. Even if they don't fully grasp that he'll be put to death and then come back to life, he still warns them ahead of time. Jesus knows they'll remember what he's told them eventually, when it begins to play out. In time, everything would make sense.

It's like that in your life too—you can't always see what's around the next corner. But Jesus can. He'll give you what you need to get where you're going, but not all at once. Sometimes it's like putting a puzzle together, one piece at a time—eventually the full picture is revealed. In the same way, God's complete plan would be shown only after Jesus's death and resurrection.

My Prayer

Dear God,
Thank you for sending Jesus to earth so I could have a relationship with you.
Amen.

Stone
for the Journey

**Jesus died
and rose so
I can live.**

Final Word

Listen! I am standing and knocking at your door. If you hear my voice and open the door, I will come in and we will eat together.

Revelation 3:20 CEV

39

Taxes or Trust

Words from the Rock

The children get off free, right? But so we don't upset them needlessly, go down to the lake, cast a hook, and pull in the first fish that bites. Open its mouth and you'll find a coin. Take it and give it to the tax men. It will be enough for both of us.

Matthew 17:26–27 Message

Jesus has just been questioned about whether or not he and his disciples paid taxes. Ironically, taxes back then were just as much of a pain (maybe more so) as taxes nowadays. In fact, most of the tax collectors were crooks who took more money than was owed.

Jesus answers the question with a question. He reminds the tax collectors that in their country, only the foreigners were supposed to pay taxes, not the locals like Jesus and his disciples. While this was essentially true, it's not how things were being done. The locals were being taxed to the hilt, and there was no way to stop it.

After Jesus makes his point that these taxes were unfair, he then says he doesn't want to make trouble. So he tells a disciple to run down to the lake and catch a fish. Now that probably seems an odd response to paying taxes, but you can almost imagine the twinkle in Jesus's eye as he adds, "Open that fish's mouth and you'll find a coin inside, which will be enough to pay our taxes." Sure enough, that's what happens.

Jesus's point in this "transaction" seems threefold. First, he makes it clear that these taxes aren't fair. In fact, there are many things in life that aren't fair. Secondly, he says it's not worth it to get in a fight over taxes. It was no big deal. And why was that? That's the third point, where the fish comes in—Jesus knows that God will provide, and we should trust God to give us what we need more than we should worry about unfair taxes.

My Prayer

Dear God,
Teach me to trust in you for all things. Even when life's not fair, help me to believe you're watching out for me.
Amen.

Stone
for the Journey

Life's not fair, but God makes up for it.

Final Word

If they obey and serve him, they will spend the rest of their days in prosperity and their years in contentment.

Job 36:11 NIV

40

Small Examples

Words from the Rock

I tell you the truth, unless you change and become like little children, you will never enter the kingdom of heaven. Therefore, whoever humbles himself like this child is the greatest in the kingdom of heaven.

Matthew 18:3–4 NIV

Who would have thought that a statement about little kids could be one of Jesus's most powerful and memorable teachings? Yet it is. Perhaps the impact comes from the fact that most people (both then and now) tend to think kids are rather insignificant and sometimes downright inconvenient. They can be noisy and obnoxious, yet they're easy to brush off, send to bed, push around. . . . After all, they're just kids.

But that's not how Jesus sees them. When he looks at little children, he sees *complete human beings*. Unlike their adult counterparts, these little people have yet to become jaded or cynical or apathetic or hopeless or prideful. Children are still young enough to be full of life and joy and faith and passion—the kinds of qualities Jesus wishes everyone could have.

Best of all, these children want to embrace Jesus. It's as if they instinctively know who he is and why he's so special. They can't wait to get close to him. In fact, that's why the disciples have been herding the kids away—so they won't "disturb" Jesus's teaching. But Jesus sees the little children as a great teaching tool for the grown-ups in the crowd. He tells his listeners to imitate them. He wants all of us to embrace his love and his gifts with eager, childlike enthusiasm.

My Prayer

Dear God,
Please help me to have a childlike heart so I'm eager and passionate when it comes to loving you.
Amen.

> **Stone**
> *for the Journey*
>
> **I will stay childlike in my love for God.**

Final Word

> *Beware that you don't look down on any of these little ones. For I tell you that in heaven their angels are always in the presence of my heavenly Father.*
>
> Matthew 18:10 NLT

Defending the Defenseless

Words from the Rock

Anyone who welcomes a little child like this on my behalf is welcoming me. But if you cause one of these little ones who trusts in me to fall into sin, it would be better for you to have a large millstone tied around your neck and be drowned in the depths of the sea.

Matthew 18:5–6 NLT

Jesus wants us to really understand how important children are. In fact, he takes it a step further by saying the way you treat a child is the way you treat him. Those are powerful words. Especially when you consider the ever-increasing rates of child abuse, child neglect, and children's health and nutrition issues both in the United States and around the world. In a way, Jesus is putting a huge responsibility on all of us to take better care of the hurting children on the planet. Jesus is the ultimate defender of the defenseless.

To this end, Jesus delivers an extremely severe warning for anyone who causes a child "to fall into sin" by saying that a child abuser would be better off drowned in the ocean. One assumption is that Jesus is talking about someone who has sexually abused a child, and there are many who think that act should result in the death penalty. But Jesus could also be referring to those who physically or verbally abuse children. Any kind of abuse might cause a child to question life, to stop trusting God, and to make poor choices. It's no wonder Jesus condemned the abuser.

Fortunately, God is able to restore our broken spirits and can heal the wounds of a messed-up childhood, if we come to him with our pain and let him. But as for the ones inflicting the pain, Jesus put it plainly—they would be better off at the bottom of the ocean.

My Prayer

Dear God,
It grieves me to think of little children suffering. Please show me what I can do to help someone who is hurting. Let me be your caring hands.
Amen.

Stone
for the Journey

God can use
me to help
the helpless.

Final Word

Blessed is he who has regard for the weak; the LORD delivers him in times of trouble. The LORD will protect him and preserve his life; he will bless him in the land and not surrender him to the desire of his foes.

Psalm 41:1–2 NIV

42

Trip Ups

Words from the Rock

The world is in for trouble because of the way it causes people to sin. There will always be something to cause people to sin, but anyone who does this will be in for trouble.

Matthew 18:7 CEV

Jesus gives everyone a stern warning here. He points out that the world in general is in trouble for the way it trips people up. However, this isn't anything new, and it's not all that surprising that Jesus is fed up. He's had run-ins with Satan from the very beginning. In fact, the reason Jesus has come to earth is to equip people to stand against the evil garbage Satan hurls at the planet on a daily basis. Even so, Jesus knows this kind of thing will continue after his earthly ministry ends. He also knows that Satan's attacks against Jesus's followers will only strengthen their commitment to God.

But Jesus's warning goes beyond saying that Satan will get his. This warning is similar to cautioning people not to harm children, but this time Jesus advises anyone who would purposely try to trip up someone else to watch out. Think about it—haven't we all done this a time or two?

In other words, Jesus is probably warning everyone. We all need to remember that sometimes a very small or seemingly insignificant thing we do could cause someone else to stumble. It could be a bad choice, refusing to listen, or being in the wrong place at the wrong time—and taking a friend along with you. Suddenly it all comes down, and you're in the hot seat with someone else pointing the finger at you. Jesus is saying not to go there. It's bad enough when you make a mistake that causes you to suffer. It's far worse when you drag someone else down with you.

My Prayer

Dear God,
Please help me never to trip someone else up. And if I do hurt someone, help me to quickly make things right and to learn from my mistake.
Amen.

> ### Stone
> *for the Journey*
>
> **I will watch my step when it comes to my life and how I lead others.**

Final Word

I've loved you the way my Father has loved me. Make yourselves at home in my love. If you keep my commands, you'll remain intimately at home in my love. That's what I've done—kept my Father's commands and made myself at home in his love.

John 15:9–10 Message

43

Just Lose It

Words from the Rock

*If your hand or your foot gets in the way of God,
chop it off and throw it away. You're better off
maimed or lame and alive than the proud owners
of two hands and two feet, godless in a furnace
of eternal fire. And if your eye distracts you from
God, pull it out and throw it away. You're better
off one-eyed and alive than exercising your twenty-
twenty vision from inside the fire of hell.*

Matthew 18:8–9 Message

Jesus's warning about sin feels very extreme here. In fact, these words are commonly misunderstood and questioned. Is Jesus really telling you to cut off your hand or your foot? Does he really want you to gouge out your eye? If Jesus loves you the way you thought he did, why would he want to make you suffer like that?

Jesus is trying to make a point, and he wants to get our attention. Discussing the possibility of chopping off body parts tends to make a person sit up and listen. But suppose that your foot really did have a mind of its own, and it decided it was a good idea to go around kicking people. And suppose it got really good at kicking people and started breaking old people's bones or knocking small children in front of buses. (Sounds kind of like a Stephen King novel.) Just suppose that really happened and you had absolutely no control over this evil foot that could take out another person. Seriously, wouldn't it be better to have that foot amputated than to let it drag you first to prison, then to death row, and eventually to hell?

Jesus is saying that if something in your life is going to drag you into sin, get rid of it. In the long run, you'll be glad you did. Hopefully it's not a body part, but maybe it's something on the Internet that's messing with your mind, maybe it's a car you drive too fast, or maybe a boyfriend who pushes you too far. Just lose whatever it is, and in the end you will save yourself.

My Prayer

Dear God,
Please help me to see if there's anything in my life that entices me to sin. Then give me the self-discipline to get rid of it.
Amen.

> ## Stone
> *for the Journey*
>
> **I will not allow sin to take root in my life.**

Final Word

> *Obey my laws and live by my decrees. I am your GOD. Keep my decrees and laws: The person who obeys them lives by them. I am GOD.*
>
> Leviticus 18:4–5 Message

44

Persistent Love

If a man has a hundred sheep and one of them wanders away, what will he do? Won't he leave the ninety-nine others on the hills and go out to search for the one that is lost? And if he finds it, I tell you the truth, he will rejoice over it more than over the ninety-nine that didn't wander away! In the same way, it is not my heavenly Father's will that even one of these little ones should perish.

Matthew 18:12–14 NLT

It's not surprising that Jesus goes from talking about sin to telling a love story. This shepherd parable is about pure love—God's determined, persistent, and unconditional love. Unless you've ever been a shepherd, you probably don't really know what's entailed in caring for sheep, but let's just say it's not a glamorous job. In Jesus's day, shepherds were regarded almost like homeless people—losers who weren't good for anything more than watching dumb sheep. Quite likely, some probably earned the name.

But there were also some good shepherds who took their jobs seriously. They cared about the sheep and made sure they had good grass to eat and clean water to drink. They protected the sheep from predators and always kept head counts. Maybe they even knew the sheep by name. For sure, if a sheep went missing, a good shepherd would go out looking. He'd climb over rough terrain, and even if it took all night, he'd search and search. He'd know better than anyone that a lone sheep was in danger of becoming dinner for a hungry wolf. And when he found the lost sheep, he'd be over the moon with happiness because he truly cared about it.

As usual, Jesus's story has more than just one point. The example of the shepherd going the distance to find the lost sheep is for us too. Sometimes we get to be like that shepherd—we get to go the extra mile to rescue someone in distress. When we do this—not so we can get attention or a pat on the back, but because we truly love and care about that person in need—we imitate Jesus, and nothing could please him more.

My Prayer

Dear God,
I want to be more like you. Show me ways that I can reach out to the lost. Give me a heart to love those in need.
Amen.

Stone
for the Journey

I can reach out to one lost person today.

Final Word

You are my hiding place! You protect me from trouble, and you put songs in my heart because you have saved me.

Psalm 32:7 CEV

Work It Out

Words from the Rock

If a fellow believer hurts you, go and tell him—work it out between the two of you. If he listens, you've made a friend. If he won't listen, take one or two others along so that the presence of witnesses will keep things honest, and try again. If he still won't listen, tell the church. If he won't listen to the church, you'll have to start over from scratch, confront him with the need for repentance, and offer again God's forgiving love.

Matthew 18:15–17 Message

Jesus knows that humans, by nature, don't really get along. Oh, things might go smoothly for a while, but eventually even the of best friends get into a dispute. Married couples have fights. Partners in business disagree. Even churches have been known to have their squabbles. So Jesus lays down some very important ground rules about relationships between Christians.

Unfortunately, many of us turn our backs on Jesus's words, tossing out these rules when it comes to settling differences. Sometimes we're more concerned about being right than making things right. So here are the rules. You might want to copy them down on an index card just in case you ever need them.

1. If a Christian does something that hurts you, go to that person and calmly tell him or her that you are hurting. Explain how his or her words or actions made you feel and why. Be honest yet kind.
2. If that person will listen, you can talk and work out your differences. That might mean taking responsibility for some of the blame. It might mean one or both of you need to forgive. But if you work things out, you have gained a true friend.
3. If that person won't listen to you, go to another Christian friend (or two) and explain the situation. But be honest and don't try to make the other person look like a jerk. There are always two sides.
4. The two or three of you should go to the other person—not to confront him or her but to speak honestly (with kindness and love) and see if you can resolve your differences. Usually this works.
5. If all that doesn't work (which is a rare case), and if you and the other person attend the same church, you can go to your church leadership and explain the situation. Then you simply start the whole process over again from step 1.

My Prayer

Dear God,
Show me how to take good care of my relationships with others. When I have a disagreement, help me to handle it correctly. Amen.

Final Word

Stone
for the Journey

God can help me to love others even when it's not easy.

> Blessed are the peacemakers, for they will be called sons of God.
>
> Matthew 5:9 NIV

46

Power Promise

Words from the Rock

I promise you that God in heaven will allow whatever you allow on earth, but he will not allow anything you don't allow. I promise that when any two of you on earth agree about something you are praying for, my Father in heaven will do it for you. Whenever two or three of you come together in my name, I am there with you.

Matthew 18:18–20 CEV

Jesus makes a powerful promise to his disciples here. It's a promise for us too, but it only works when we're connected to Jesus. In other words, we can't do this on our own—the power comes directly from God, and Jesus is the transmitter. For us to imagine our words can make their way to heaven or that we can receive what we pray for—without being connected to Jesus—is like a table lamp bragging that it can illuminate a room without being plugged into an electrical outlet.

But when we remain connected to Jesus—praying to him, believing in him, experiencing his life in us—we will have this kind of power.

We will be able to say and do things on earth that Jesus will stamp with his approval in heaven. We can get together with other believers and pray for God to do miraculous things, and we can be sure that God will do them. He's God and knows what's best, so he'll do what we ask in his time and in his way, but he will definitely move.

Perhaps the best part of this promise is that Jesus assures us that when we get together with other believers (even if it's only two or three) and our main purpose in being together is Jesus—if we're there to worship him, pray to him, learn more about him, or study his Word—then he will be right there with us. And when he is, we can be sure he'll be the one guiding our prayers and our words. We'll experience his answers to our prayers because of our connection to him.

My Prayer

Dear God,
Thank you for promising so much power to me. Remind me that the power comes from you and that I must be connected to Jesus to receive it.
Amen.

> ### Stone
> *for the Journey*
>
> **Powerful miracles happen when I'm connected to God.**

Final Word

If my people, who are called by my name, will humble themselves and pray and seek my face and turn from their wicked ways, then will I hear from heaven and will forgive their sin and will heal their land.

2 Chronicles 7:14 NIV

47

Forgive and Forgive

Words from the Rock

No, not seven times . . . but seventy times seven!

Matthew 18:22 NLT

You may have heard these numbers before. This is Jesus's response to Peter's question about how many times he should forgive a person. Maybe someone had offended Peter and he was getting tired of forgiving the same person again and again. So when Peter tossed out the number seven, he probably thought he was being generous. But Jesus comes back and multiplies seven by seventy, which really means you should always forgive—no limits.

To drive home his point, Jesus tells a parable about a rich man who had loaned out a lot of money and decided he wanted it back. One of the debts he wanted to collect was about a million dollars, but the guy who owed it was flat broke. So the rich man said he'd foreclose on all the deadbeat's properties (houses and livestock) and throw him in debtors prison. But the broke guy got on his knees and begged and pleaded, and the rich man actually had mercy, forgiving him his million-dollar debt!

Then this same man (who'd barely escaped foreclosure and prison) went to a guy who owed him about a hundred bucks and ordered this dude to pay up. And when the poor guy couldn't pay it all, the first guy (the one who'd just been forgiven a million-dollar debt) had him thrown in prison.

You can imagine how the rich man must have felt when he heard about this. How dare this man, who'd been forgiven a million-dollar debt, be so harsh and greedy as to throw someone into prison for something so small! Jesus tells Peter that's how God feels when we refuse to forgive others after God has so generously forgiven us.

My Prayer

Dear God,
Help me to remember how much you have forgiven me, and help me to be quick to forgive (again and again) anyone who offends me.
Amen.

Stone
for the Journey

Because of God, there is no limit to forgiveness.

Final Word

Put up with each other, and forgive anyone who does you wrong, just as Christ has forgiven you.

Colossians 3:13 CEV

48

Marriage Plan

Words from the Rock

Haven't you read . . . that at the beginning the Creator "made them male and female," and said, "For this reason a man will leave his father and mother and be united to his wife, and the two will become one flesh"? So they are no longer two, but one. Therefore what God has joined together, let man not separate.

Matthew 19:4–6 NIV

The Pharisees have just questioned Jesus about divorce. As usual, they're trying to trap him up in their own mishmash of religious rules, probably hoping to publicly embarrass him. But, as usual, Jesus doesn't fall for their trickery. Instead he gives them a quick refresher course on God's best plan for marriage, quoting from an ancient Scripture that these "learned" men should recognize.

It's reassuring to hear Jesus remind everyone that God really did plan for marriage way back at the beginning of time. And the plan was really so simple. God made two genders—male and female—who would grow to an age at which they were old enough to support themselves separately from their parents. At that point the man and woman would marry and become "one flesh." They would join together not only physically and sexually but also emotionally, mentally, fiscally, and socially. "They are no longer two, but one." The focus is on joining two people, man and woman, to create something lasting.

But the real key is found in the last sentence: "What God has joined together, let man not separate." The key word is *God*. For a marriage to endure the test of time, God must become part of the equation (one man + one woman = marriage). If God is part of a courtship and marriage, and if the marriage relationship is built on God's rock-solid foundation (love, forgiveness, honesty, faithfulness), then no human will be able to blow the marriage apart.

Because God has such respect for marriage, he wants for you to respect him in the relationships you have *before* marriage. God knows that the way you handle your dating life (for better or for worse) will later impact your marriage, and he wants you to have the best marriage possible. So if you date, why not invite God to join you? After all, he's there with you anyway.

My Prayer

Dear God,
I believe my life and future are in your hands.
If that includes marriage, I trust that you'll lead me and show me what's best for me.
Amen.

Stone
for the Journey

Only God can plan a marriage that will endure.

Final Word

For the grace of God has been revealed, bringing salvation to all people. And we are instructed to turn from godless living and sinful pleasures. We should live in this evil world with wisdom, righteousness, and devotion to God.

Titus 2:11–12 NLT

Hard Hearts

> *Moses permitted you to divorce your wives because your hearts were hard. But it was not this way from the beginning. I tell you that anyone who divorces his wife, except for marital unfaithfulness, and marries another woman commits adultery.*
>
> Matthew 19:8–9 NIV

The Pharisees don't let Jesus off the hook after his refresher course on marriage. They come right back at him, demanding to know why Moses allowed legal divorces so many years ago, if marriage is designed by God. Their plan is still to trip up Jesus, but he turns their plan against them to show what they're really thinking.

Jesus is aware of the trend of religious leaders abusing the old divorce law as an excuse to get rid of an unwanted wife. It's just another one of their nasty little legal loopholes they use to get what they want (in this case, probably a younger, prettier wife). Consequently, Jesus delivers his answer directly to the Pharisees, saying the only reason they're permitted to divorce is because their hearts are so hard, and that divorce only becomes an option if a spouse has been unfaithful. And even in that case, he warns, a remarriage is considered adultery.

Naturally, this isn't what the Pharisees want to hear. They probably stomp off mad. Jesus nailed it when he said their hearts were hard. It was, in fact, the hardness of their hypocritical hearts that spoiled not only their marriages but everything they touched. It made them bitterly jealous of Jesus, and sadly, it blinded them to the fact that the God they supposedly served was doing something amazing right in front of them.

Hearts sometimes get hardened when our plans don't match up with God's. That's why he invites us to stay in relationship with him, so that our plans can align with his and our hearts can remain soft.

My Prayer

Dear God,
I know a hardened heart is like being blind and falling down flat on my face. Please let me never harden my heart toward you.
Amen.

Stone
for the Journey

**I will trust
God's perfect
plan for
my life.**

Final Word

When tempted, no one should say, "God is tempting me." For God cannot be tempted by evil, nor does he tempt anyone.

James 1:13 NIV

Single Hearts

Words from the Rock

Only those people who have been given the gift of staying single can accept this teaching. Some people are unable to marry because of birth defects or because of what someone has done to their bodies. Others stay single for the sake of the kingdom of heaven. Anyone who can accept this teaching should do so.

Matthew 19:11–12 CEV

After Jesus answers the Pharisees about divorce, his disciples grow concerned and say, "If that's how it is between a man and a woman, it's better not to get married" (v. 10 CEV). You can almost hear the fear in their voices. It's no wonder, since the disciples (from varied homes and backgrounds) have suspected their lives would change as a result of following Jesus. Most are single, and some are married but away from their wives. Ones like Peter, in light of his call to ministry, might have been questioning the practicality of marriage in general.

Jesus gently but honestly answers them, saying that some people *do* have the gift of remaining single and that they would surely agree with what the disciples have just suggested. He also points out that some people don't marry because of the way they are, while some will stay single for reasons of faith. Obviously, based on his other teachings, Jesus believes many will find it best to marry.

Basically, Jesus is saying that everyone's situation, each one's path, will be different. We each have to figure out what God's best plan is for us. We shouldn't tell someone else how to live his or her life. Jesus obviously knew that the early church would begin after his death and resurrection, and he must have suspected marriage would be just one of the issues they would grapple with. Even so, Jesus doesn't lay down the law—that's not who he is. He simply speaks the truth, suggesting that each of us will have to figure out which is right for us—staying single or being married. It's between us and God.

My Prayer

Dear God,
Whether you want me to remain single or get married someday, I want to do what you want me to. Please show me your perfect will for my life.
Amen.

Stone
for the Journey

God will lead me down the path he has chosen for me.

Final Word

You followed my teaching, conduct, purpose, faith, patience, love, perseverance.

2 Timothy 3:10 NASB

51

Not Enough

Words from the Rock

A man stopped Jesus and asked, "Teacher, what good thing must I do to get eternal life?"

Jesus said, "Why do you question me about what's good? God is the One who is good. If you want to enter the life of God, just do what he tells you."

The man asked, "What in particular?"

Jesus said, "Don't murder, don't commit adultery, don't steal, don't lie, honor your father and mother, and love your neighbor as you do yourself."

The young man said, "I've done all that. What's left?"

"If you want to give it all you've got," Jesus replied, "go sell your possessions; give everything to the poor. All your wealth will then be in heaven. Then come follow me."

That was the last thing the young man expected to hear. And so, crest-fallen, he walked away. He was holding on tight to a lot of things, and he couldn't bear to let go.

Matthew 19:16–22 Message

This Scripture begins on a hopeful note. A young man approaches Jesus for advice on how to get eternal life. Yet this confident young man almost seems to have a hidden agenda—which, naturally, Jesus will see through and expose. In fact, right from the start Jesus counters with "Why not just go directly to God? He's good and will tell you what to do." But the young man wants specifics. So Jesus starts rattling off commandments, then waits for a response. The persistent young man announces that he's done all that and asks what else he must do.

Imagine Jesus in that moment. Does he pause hopefully, or does he already know the outcome? Whatever the case, he asks the man the big question—is he willing to give up everything? Can he sell all his belongings, give the money to the poor, and follow Jesus? Sadly, the answer is no. The reason? This young man is wealthy—he has many possessions, and he's not willing to part with them. Not even for Jesus.

If only he knew what he had given up . . . or maybe he does, and that's why he goes away sad. He rejects an eternal treasure that would only increase in value in order to hold on to his earthly "riches" that are worthless.

God wants us to realize and appreciate the difference between things this world values (like money, cars, clothes), and what he offers (like a fulfilled life, endless love, enduring peace). He wants us to choose what's most valuable and hold onto it.

My Prayer

Dear God,
I don't ever want my attachment to things to keep me from serving you. Please remind me of what's really valuable and what's not.
Amen.

> **Stone**
> *for the Journey*
>
> **The best I can do is to follow God.**

Final Word

> *Don't be greedy! Owning a lot of things won't make your life safe.*
>
> Luke 12:15 CEV

Stumbling Block

> *I tell you the truth, it will be hard for a rich person to enter the kingdom of heaven. Yes, I tell you that it is easier for a camel to go through the eye of a needle than for a rich person to enter the kingdom of God.*
>
> Matthew 19:23–24 NCV

*M*ost people just scratch their heads at the image of a camel going through the eye of a needle. It sounds crazy-impossible. But it could be that Jesus was really describing a particular entrance into the walled city of Jerusalem.

It seems that, due to security reasons, the only way to enter the city late at night was via an inconvenient entry that had been designed to prevent enemy invasions. The entrance was more like a large hole in the wall, big enough for people to pass through one by one. Perhaps a small, well-mannered, coordinated donkey—if it wasn't carrying a load—might be enticed to step through. But a camel—ridiculous.

Keep in mind that camels were usually the transportation of the very wealthy (like royalty or merchants), and they were usually loaded down with lots of valuable possessions. If it were even possible to get a large, awkward, and possibly ill-tempered camel to climb through this passageway (and that's assuming a lot), its rider would still have to unload all those expensive goods, setting them on the darkened street where bandits could be lurking. Then imagine as this frustrated rich man attempts to shove, push, or pull his camel through the tight hole. And what if the camel got stuck?

The point to all this? Jesus is saying that riches (money and material possessions) can be a stumbling block to anyone. What you love becomes your master. If you love material stuff more than Jesus, you will serve those things more than you serve Jesus. Which would you rather give your life to?

My Prayer

Dear God,
Help me to keep you as my number one priority. If material possessions ever distract me from loving you, please give me the strength to get rid of them.
Amen.

Stone
for the Journey

I choose to love God more than anything else.

Final Word

Keep your lives free from the love of money and be content with what you have, because God has said, "Never will I leave you; never will I forsake you."

Hebrews 13:5 NIV

53

Impossible Possibilities

Words from the Rock

With man this is impossible, but with God all things are possible.

Matthew 19:26 NIV

*T*his is a promise you can cling to—and maybe even memorize for the times you need an encouraging reminder—when you're faced with a challenge that seems impossible. And you'll have lots of impossible challenges if you're trying to live out your faith—that's just the way it goes. But if you're trying to live out your faith *without* God's help, it will be hopelessly impossible. Any attempt to live as a Christian without God isn't just futile, it's pathetic—not to mention foolish.

Imagine you're pretty good at basketball (maybe you are), and your big dream is to get really good. Yet for some reason you try to do this from your bedroom. Maybe you play basketball via a computer game or you have an old Nerf basketball with a hoop attached to your laundry basket. You stay in your room spending hours just shooting away, but your game's not getting better. Then imagine (okay, this takes some big imagination) that your last name is Jordan and your dad's name is Michael. He just happens to be a retired NBA star who's been waiting to play some one-on-one with you, but you're too busy "practicing" in your room to go downstairs to the big indoor gymnasium with real hoops and shoot with your dad. Get the picture?

That's kind of how silly it would be for you to try to do this Christian walk on your own without God's help. It is humanly impossible, but with God all things are possible. He's right there, always ready and waiting to help you with your game.

My Prayer

Dear God,
Remind me not to get discouraged when something feels impossible, but to simply come to you and ask for help. All things are possible with you!
Amen.

> **Stone**
> *for the Journey*
>
> **I need God to accomplish the impossible.**

Final Word

> *Let us hold tightly without wavering to the hope we affirm, for God can be trusted to keep his promise.*
>
> Hebrews 10:23 NLT

Great Benefits

Words from the Rock

Yes, you have followed me. In the re-creation of the world, when the Son of Man will rule gloriously, you who have followed me will also rule. . . . And not only you, but anyone who sacrifices home, family, fields—whatever—because of me will get it all back a hundred times over, not to mention the considerable bonus of eternal life. This is the Great Reversal: many of the first ending up last, and the last first.

Matthew 19:28–30 Message

Jesus's disciples have pretty much given up everything to follow Jesus. They've left families, jobs, and homes just to be with Jesus, to learn from him, and to help with his ministry. At this stage, they might be wondering if it's really going to be worth what they've sacrificed. In fact, they have just asked Jesus that very thing—what will they get out of this?

This promise is Jesus's answer for his disciples. But it's also for all believers who will come later, who will love God enough to put him in that first-place position in their hearts—in essence, giving up everything to follow and serve him.

Jesus promises that whatever you give up for him will be returned to you a hundred times over—and that isn't even counting the promise of eternal life, which is returned about a million times over. In other words, he's saying you'll never be sorry that you chose to follow him. Sure, there will be times when life's hard or challenging, but holding fast to God will always be worth the effort. He promises to make it worth everything you give up and a lot more—not necessarily in your earthly life, although having God's presence in your daily life is better than anything. But Jesus promises that eternal life will be so incredible your earthly mind can't even begin to comprehend it.

My Prayer

Dear God,
Thank you for all that you have for me. Remind me that what I give up for you now is not only in my best interest, but it will be repaid again and again throughout eternity.
Amen.

> **Stone**
> *for the Journey*
>
> **I cannot outgive God.**

Final Word

If you give to others, you will be given a full amount in return. It will be packed down, shaken together, and spilling over into your lap. The way you treat others is the way you will be treated.

Luke 6:38 CEV

First and Last

55

Words from the Rock

God's kingdom is like an estate manager who went out early in the morning to hire workers for his vineyard. They agreed on a [very generous] wage of a dollar a day, and went to work. Later, about nine o'clock, the manager saw some other men hanging around the town square unemployed. He told them to go to work in his vineyard and he would pay them a fair wage. They went.

[The manager randomly hired workers like that into the afternoon, all for a dollar a day, and when the day ended and it was time to pay the workers, they all got the same pay, whether they'd worked all day or an hour. This made the ones who'd worked all day angry.]

[The manager] replied to the one speaking for the rest, "Friend, I haven't been unfair. We agreed on the wage of a dollar, didn't we? So take it and go. I decided to give to the one who came last the same as you. Can't I do what I want with my own money? Are you going to get stingy because I am generous?"

Matthew 20:1–5, 13–15 Message

This parable confuses and frustrates a lot of people, probably because it goes against almost everything our culture has taught us about work ethic. We believe in an honest wage for an honest day's work, but this parable is saying something altogether different. In a nutshell, some guys worked for an hour, while others worked for a full day, and they all got paid exactly the same.

So imagine you're desperate for a job. Times are hard, your children are starving, and you're about to lose your home. You're willing to do anything for a buck. You feel jealous when you see others working. Why can't that be you?

The day is almost done, your stomach is growling, and you know your kids will go to bed hungry again. Then, to your surprise, the field manager offers you work—and you'll receive a full day's wages! You can hardly believe it, and you jump in and work as hard as you can right up until sunset. You're so thankful that you wish you could have worked longer.

Jesus uses this story to show how people live their earthly lives. Some will spend a lifetime knowing, loving, and serving him. Others will spend most of their lives struggling to get along, making mistakes, and feeling spiritually lost. But as long as they all find their way into a relationship with God, whether early in life or at the very end of it, they will all get the same reward—eternal life! Why should anyone be resentful of that? Shouldn't we all be happy for everyone who receives eternal life?

My Prayer

Dear God,
I'm so thankful to have found you early in life.
Help me to be gracious to anyone who takes longer.
Amen.

> **Stone**
> *for the Journey*
>
> **I will not question God's generosity toward me or others.**

Final Word

Here it is again, the Great Reversal: many of the first ending up last, and the last first.

Matthew 20:16 Message

56

Headed to the Cross

Words from the Rock

We are now on our way to Jerusalem, where the Son of Man will be handed over to the chief priests and the teachers of the Law of Moses. They will sentence him to death, and then they will hand him over to foreigners who will make fun of him. They will beat him and nail him to a cross. But on the third day he will rise from death.

Matthew 20:18–19 CEV

*A*gain Jesus is predicting his death. Only this time he's much more specific about the details. Jesus and his disciples are on their way to Jerusalem when he makes this disclosure. He tells them privately because it's not time for anyone else to hear. Interestingly, we don't get to see or hear their reaction to this announcement. Maybe they were very quiet, trying to process what Jesus was saying. Or maybe they were in disbelief, wondering how all that could happen. Or perhaps they were simply in shock, hoping beyond hope that Jesus was wrong about this. Whatever the case, no conversation is recorded to show their reaction.

What would your reaction be if you'd been there that day? How would it feel to hear Jesus saying these things? First he was going be handed over to those hypocritical religious leaders that no one really liked or respected? Who was going to hand him over? Then he would be sentenced to death? For doing what? And then he would be ridiculed by foreigners? How could that possibly happen?

But then it gets even grimmer—Jesus would be beaten and nailed to the cross? That was how criminals were put to death. Could you even bear to think of that? And finally, after three days, he would return to life? How was that even possible?

Maybe you would have been quiet too, just trying to wrap your head around all this dismal information and hoping it wasn't really going to happen. But how do you feel about it now, knowing that it did happen? It all went down just as Jesus had predicted. And it happened like that so God could extend his love and forgiveness to everyone, including you. How do you respond to that?

My Prayer

Dear God,
Thank you for sending Jesus to earth and for his willingness to die so I could have eternal life. I never want to take that gift for granted.
Amen.

> # Stone
> *for the Journey*
>
> **I'm thankful that Jesus went to the cross for me.**

Final Word

For God so loved the world that he gave his one and only Son, that whoever believes in him shall not perish but have eternal life.

John 3:16 NIV

Who's on Top?

Words from the Rock

You know that the rulers in this world lord it over their people, and officials flaunt their authority over those under them. But among you it will be different. Whoever wants to be a leader among you must be your servant, and whoever wants to be first among you must become your slave. For even the Son of Man came not to be served but to serve others and to give his life as a ransom for many.

Matthew 20:25–28 NLT

Jesus says a lot of things that are hard to understand—at least at first. It often seems he's coming from a completely different direction. Or maybe he's just coming from heaven. But in this section he tells his disciples (and all who would follow him) that his way of measuring leadership is exactly the opposite of the way the world does it.

Think about it—if people want to be elected to positions of leadership, they make themselves known. Often they spend money to do this, campaigning for votes. They go hang with other "important" people. They get their picture in the news, and they hold fancy fundraisers where only the rich get invited. It's pretty much in-your-face, and sometimes it's obnoxious.

Jesus says that if you really want to be a leader, you should act like a servant. A servant is someone who takes care of others, who cleans up other people's messes, who puts the needs of someone else over his or her own. It's not a glamorous job. Even less glamorous is the life of a slave. But Jesus says that if you really want to be on top, you need to be a slave. A slave can't even call his life his own. He's at the beck and call of someone else. The needs of his master and everyone else come before his own.

When you think about it, that's exactly what Jesus did. He left his kingdom in heaven to come to earth and take care of us, clean up our messes, put our needs above his own . . . and to eventually be put to death on the cross, which must have seemed like hitting rock bottom to some. But now he rules and reigns with God in heaven forever—from the bottom straight to the top. And he wants us to imitate him by humbling ourselves and being willing to serve like he did—that way he can be the one to lift us up.

My Prayer

Dear God,
Help me to see the value of being a servant.
Show me ways I can put others' needs above
my own. Make me more like you.
Amen.

Stone
for the Journey

**Jesus can
teach me how
to be a servant.**

Final Word

Each one must do just as he has purposed in his heart, not grudgingly or under compulsion, for God loves a cheerful giver.

2 Corinthians 9:7 NASB

58

Sealed Fates

I will be with you a little while longer. Then I will go back to the One who sent me. You will look for me, but you will not find me. And you cannot come where I am.

John 7:33–34 NCV

Jesus is in the temple when he makes this announcement. He says it loudly enough for all to hear, but he's directing it to the religious leaders who have just confronted him and are now attempting to have him arrested. Naturally, his words confuse these "educated" men. They can only assume that Jesus must be putting together some kind of devious plot to overthrow them. They even begin to fret that Jesus plans to take his teaching abroad, perhaps to the Jews who live in foreign lands. That is a huge concern to them. What if his ministry would expand? What if he would influence Jews to abandon their religion for his "heresy"?

Yet there are others in the temple who are growing increasingly interested in Jesus. They've seen some of his miracles and heard some of his teaching, and they're beginning to ask themselves if this man might truly be the Messiah. Of course, this only makes the religious leaders more fearful and jealous, and this drives them toward the final chapter of Jesus's earthly life.

It seems pretty obvious what Jesus is saying to these religious leaders. He's telling them that he's going back to the one who sent him—his Father. He already told them they don't know his Father. Now Jesus is saying they won't be able to find him once he's gone. Furthermore, they won't be able to go where he's going—simply because they have refused to believe that he is God's Son. They have rejected Jesus, and as a result, they have rejected the very same God they thought they'd been serving. They are sealing their own spiritual fate.

But Jesus has revealed himself to you. You know why he came to earth, what he did, and where he has gone. He wants you to believe in him so that one day you can join him in heaven. Where the unbelievers sealed their fate by dismissing Jesus, you seal your fate by believing in him.

My Prayer

Dear God,
I don't ever want to be like the Pharisees, rejecting you and the one who sent you. Thank you for sealing my fate with you so I can join you in heaven.
Amen.

Final Word

> *In this fellowship we enjoy the eternal life he promised us.*
>
> 1 John 2:25 NLT

Stone
for the Journey

I will be welcome in heaven because of my relationship with Jesus.

Thirst Quencher

Words from the Rock

Anyone who is thirsty may come to me! Anyone who believes in me may come and drink! For the Scriptures declare, "Rivers of living water will flow from his heart."

John 7:37–38 NLT

Jesus makes this declaration loudly, in the presence of the crowds of people who've come to Jerusalem to celebrate the Festival of Booths (a harvest celebration). His words capture the people's attention because he's quoting from one of the prophets who had predicted the coming of the Messiah. Suddenly some of the people seem to get it. They become excited, thinking Jesus is the real deal—he's the Messiah! Oh, how they have longed for the Messiah. They have thirsted for him like people lost in the desert. And they assume that Jesus will be the one to deliver them from their oppressors (primarily the Roman government occupying their country). They're ecstatic.

Others are wary. It's not that they wouldn't welcome the Messiah—and maybe they're a little bit thirsty. But among themselves they question Jesus's bold claim. They say doubtful things like, "How can

Jesus be the Messiah if he's from Galilee?" and "Wasn't the Messiah supposed to be from the line of David?" and "The Messiah should have been born in Bethlehem, just like King David." Soon the people are arguing. Too bad they hadn't done their homework, or they would have known that Jesus was a descendant of King David and had been born in Bethlehem. Instead they rely on their own opinions and misinformation.

As the arguments grow louder, the religious leaders grow more agitated and concerned. They have absolutely no thirst for the truth or for Jesus. The only thing on their minds is, *How can we shut Jesus up for good?* They want him to be arrested and locked up, but it's not time for that yet. Although each day brings Jesus closer to his date with the cross, there's still work to be done. He knows that people are thirsty and growing thirstier each day, and he wants to give as much living water as possible in the time he has left for his ministry.

In the same way, he wants you to thirst for him. He wants you to know that only his love and truth can really quench your parched soul.

My Prayer

> **Stone**
> *for the Journey*
>
> **Only Jesus can quench my thirsting soul.**

Dear God,
Sometimes there's a yearning deep inside me, but I don't realize it's a thirst for you. Remind me that you are the Living Water and when I come to you, I will be filled up.
Amen.

Final Word

I heard a loud shout from the throne, saying, "Look, God's home is now among his people! He will live with them, and they will be his people. God himself will be with them."

Revelation 21:3 NLT

60

Throwing Stones

Words from the Rock

When they kept on questioning him, he straightened up and said to them, "If any one of you is without sin, let him be the first to throw a stone at her." Again he stooped down and wrote on the ground.

At this, those who heard began to go away one at a time, the older ones first, until only Jesus was left, with the woman still standing there. Jesus straightened up and asked her, "Woman, where are they? Has no one condemned you?"

"No one, sir," she said.

"Then neither do I condemn you," Jesus declared. "Go now and leave your life of sin."

John 8:7–11 NIV

The religious leaders are at it again, plotting and planning, and now they think they have Jesus between a rock and a hard place. They've caught a woman in the act of adultery. They drag her to where Jesus is teaching and throw her down in front of him and everyone else.

The Pharisees know Jewish law requires this woman to be put to death by the throwing of stones. They also know that Jesus teaches forgiveness. But how can he break Jewish law by forgiving an obviously guilty woman? To these men, it seems a cut-and-dried case, so they demand an answer from him: "What do you say?" (v. 5 NIV).

Jesus just stoops down and writes on the ground with his finger. They keep hammering at him, demanding that the woman be stoned. So he stands and says those unforgettable words: "If any one of you is without sin, let him be the first to throw a stone at her." Then he stoops down again, and one by one everyone slips away. No rocks are thrown. Because, after all, who hasn't sinned? And how gracious was Jesus? He didn't stare or point an accusing finger at the people. Yet he makes his point. Everyone has sinned.

So what gives one person the right to condemn another? Jesus didn't condemn anyone. He just told the woman to leave her life of sin behind. What a lesson that is for us—to be willing to admit that sin does exist, but without condemning a person for being a sinner. And if you think about it, when are you most eager to toss an accusation at someone else—could it be those times when you don't want someone else to accuse you?

My Prayer

Dear God,
Remind me that it's not my job to point the finger at someone else's mistakes. Let me imitate you in how you love and forgive others. Amen.

Final Word

> There is only one Lawgiver and Judge, the one who is able to save and destroy. But you—who are you to judge your neighbor?
>
> James 4:12 NIV

Stone
for the Journey

I will deal with my own faults instead of pointing out faults in others.

61

Life Light

Words from the Rock

I am the light of the world. The person who follows me will never live in darkness but will have the light that gives life.

John 8:12 NCV

People are naturally drawn to light. Whether it's sun seeking on a warm beach or star gazing on a dark night, gazing at a flickering candle in a dim room or staring into a crackling campfire, we are attracted to light. It offers warmth and comfort and illumination. Without light, this world would be a cold, dark place, and we would quickly cease to exist.

Jesus's light is not all that different. It too is a source of warmth, comfort, and illumination. Without Jesus's light, our hearts grow cold, our spirits grow uneasy, and we can't see where we're going, so we end up stumbling around. Despite all that, we still manage to shield ourselves from Jesus's light sometimes. Maybe it's in the form of spiritual sunglasses, which dim the brightness just enough so we don't have to see that certain sin area in our lives that needs attention. Or maybe it's a like a dimmer switch that somehow makes a dirty room appear more attractive. Everyone has ways of pushing Jesus's light away.

What happens when you live in a continually light-deprived condition? In your physical life, a number of things can occur as a result of the absence of sunlight—things like bone deterioration, invasion of germs and bacteria, or just plain old gloomy depression in the form of SAD (seasonal affective disorder). Your spiritual life is not so different. So if you want to be healthy and happy, soak in Jesus's light. If you don't want to stumble and fall down, let Jesus illuminate your path. Let the light shine in!

My Prayer

Dear God,
Please shine your light on me. I know I need it to find my way and to be healthy and happy. Teach me to welcome your light always.
Amen.

Stone
for the Journey

God's light brings life.

Final Word

You are a chosen people. You are royal priests, a holy nation, God's very own possession. As a result, you can show others the goodness of God, for he called you out of the darkness into his wonderful light.

1 Peter 2:9 NLT

Earthbound Minds

Words from the Rock

I know where I came from and where I am going, but you don't know this about me. You judge me by human standards, but I do not judge anyone. And if I did, my judgment would be correct in every respect because I am not alone. The Father who sent me is with me.

John 8:14–16 NLT

Although Jesus is talking to those thickheaded Pharisees, he could be talking to any of us since we're all a little dense at times, especially when it comes to grasping spiritual concepts. That's probably because we often try to understand spiritual things with our human, earthly minds, which is kind of like trying to use an old-fashioned television to receive HDTV. That old television's technology is too limited to receive the high-definition signals being transmitted. Without an adaptor, when it comes to catching anything from the airwaves, that old TV is pretty much useless.

That's how we are when we try to comprehend who Jesus is within the limitations of our earthly minds. It just doesn't work. And when we refuse to listen with our spiritual ears, we, like the Pharisees, are subject to doubt, skepticism, and cynicism. Think about it—isn't that how most nonbelievers react to Jesus? Spirituality does not compute within the confines of an earthbound mind.

But here's the good news: Jesus gets this, and he promises he won't judge us for being human (though he could if he wanted since he's connected to God, who's the highest and fairest judge in the universe). Jesus understands our human condition because he walked around the planet in human skin long enough to know how it feels. He won't judge us for being thickheaded at times.

By the same token, Jesus warns us not to judge him according to our human standards, because he knows that just won't work. Instead, he wants us to begin reasoning with our spiritual senses. And that involves faith. Don't forget that we don't need a huge amount of faith. Like Jesus said, even faith the size of a mustard seed can do miracles—as long as we plant our faith in him.

My Prayer

Dear God,
I realize that I tend to use my earthbound brain more than I use my spiritual senses. Please help me to develop a stronger spiritual sense so that I will better understand in my heart who you are and what you're up to.
Amen.

Stone
for the Journey

My spiritual senses are limited only by my earthbound mind.

Final Word

No one can explain how a baby breathes before it is born. So how can anyone explain what God does? After all, he created everything.

Ecclesiastes 11:5 CEV

63

Seeing Jesus

Words from the Rock

You're looking right at me and you don't see me. How do you expect to see the Father? If you knew me, you would at the same time know the Father.

John 8:19 Message

Jesus has just informed the religious leaders that he speaks to them on behalf of his Father. He reminds these legalistic men that even in their own court, they require two testimonies as evidence, so he tells them that he and his Father are providing them with two testimonies. Naturally, this answer doesn't please them, so in another effort to trap him, they demand to know where his Father is. Once again, he doesn't answer according to their expectations. Remember, they're locked in their earthbound minds.

Jesus plainly tells them that even though they're looking directly at him, they still can't see him. Now they're probably thinking, *Are you nuts? Of course we can see you, you're standing right there.* But they can only see him with their earthly eyes. Their spiritual eyes are blind or shut because they clearly aren't seeing Jesus for who he is.

They don't get that he's the Son of God. They don't know Jesus—who he really is—and that simply proves they don't know God.

So how does that relate to you? What's your reaction when you "see" Jesus? Keep in mind that there are many ways to see him. Sometimes you see him working in someone else, but perhaps it makes you uncomfortable. Sometimes you see him through something as basic as nature, like a beautiful sunset trying to remind you to praise God. Sometimes you see him when you're reading God's Word and a certain sentence really grabs you, or you're praying and you get a sense that God is telling you to take a certain action. When you see Jesus like this, do you always recognize him? Do you always respond?

My Prayer

> Dear God,
> Please forgive me for the times I've "seen" you but then turned away. Help me to see what you want me to see and to respond in a way that pleases you.
> Amen.

Stone
for the Journey

My spiritual eyes hunger to see God.

Final Word

> *Be sure to fear the LORD and serve him faithfully with all your heart; consider what great things he has done for you.*
>
> 1 Samuel 12:24 NIV

64

Who's a Pharisee?

Words from the Rock

You people are from here below, but I am from above. You belong to this world, but I don't belong to this world. So I told you that you would die in your sins. Yes, you will die in your sins if you don't believe that I am he.

John 8:23–24 NCV

Do you ever wonder why so many of Jesus's words recorded in the Bible were directed to those stubborn, prideful, hardhearted, thickheaded Pharisees? Why did Jesus "waste" so much time on the men who not only refused to believe in him but eventually sought to have him killed? Why would Jesus do that?

Could it be that Pharisee–type people are somewhat universal? Is it possible that all of us have a bit of Pharisee trapped inside? If you don't agree, consider some of the common negative characteristics of the typical Pharisee in Jesus's time: (1) They thought they knew more than anyone else. (2) They believed playing by their own rules would ensure their success. (3) They were certain they were superior to everyone. (4) They questioned anyone who didn't agree with them. (5) They were selfish and greedy.

Now ask yourself, *Do any of those descriptions fit me?* Who doesn't think they know more than others at times? Who wouldn't like to play by their own rules? And so on. See, we all fall into the Pharisee category sometimes. It's likely Jesus knew that, and that's probably the reason so many of his words, though aimed at the Pharisees, can be applied to anyone. So Jesus keeps it simple. In this Scripture he bluntly tells the Pharisees (and all of us) that unless they believe in Jesus and believe that he's going to die for their sins, they will die.

My Prayer

Dear God,
I confess that I sometimes act like a Pharisee, like when I think I know more than anyone else. Help me to see myself for what I am, and then let me come to you to be changed.
Amen.

> **Stone**
> *for the Journey*
>
> **I will humble myself so that God can change me.**

Final Word

> The one who is the greatest among you must become like the youngest, and the leader like the servant.
>
> Luke 22:26 NASB

65

Authorized by God

> *When you lift up the Son of Man, you will know*
> *that I am he. You will know that these things I do*
> *are not by my own authority but that I say only*
> *what the Father has taught me. The One who sent*
> *me is with me. I always do what is pleasing to him,*
> *so he has not left me alone.*

John 8:28–29 NCV

Even though Jesus was the Messiah, the chosen one, and God's own Son—which means he's actually the same as God—he still understood that his life on earth was authorized by God. In other words, he knew that any power he had on earth came directly from God. He accepted that all he knew had been given to him by God, and he respected that all he did was a direct result of God's authorization. Jesus was totally aware of this amazing and powerful connection, and he never tried to function without God's authority. So why would anyone?

Yet we do. We live "unauthorized" lives when we try to get by without God. Maybe it's not intentional, but we do it just the same.

There are times when we think we have enough strength or brains or resources or whatever, and we attempt to proceed through our lives without any assistance from God.

Even if we do manage to stumble through, we have to ask ourselves, how lame is that? Especially when we consider that God is just waiting for us to call on him, to connect ourselves to him, so that he can use his authority to direct us through life. Yet we continually come up with excuses to keep him at arm's length. Maybe we just have to learn the hard way.

We need to remember that Jesus, the Son of God, never tried to do anything on his own. He knew that he needed God's authority with him every minute of the day and every single step of the way. Jesus *never* took God's authority for granted. Why would we want to live life any differently?

My Prayer

Dear God,
I admit that I often leave you out of certain things. I'm not even sure why. Please remind me that I need you. Help me to remain connected to you and to notice what a difference your authority makes in my life. Amen.

Stone
for the Journey

To make my life really work, I must be authorized by God.

Final Word

> For God has not given us a spirit of timidity, but of power and love and discipline.
>
> 2 Timothy 1:7 NASB

66

Real Freedom

If you continue in My word, then you are truly disciples of Mine; and you will know the truth, and the truth will make you free.

John 8:31–32 NASB

*W*ho doesn't long for freedom? There's a place inside of everyone that just wants to be free.

Sometimes you may get confused over what freedom really means. Maybe you think it's a day off from your normal routines and responsibilities. Or maybe you think it's getting something for nothing. Or maybe it's sliding through a situation where you should've been nailed—getting home free.

The freedom Jesus is talking about is a lot bigger and a lot more lasting than those things. It's a soul-deep sort of freedom that feels like a load's been lifted from your shoulders. It eases your conscience and helps you to sleep better. And it basically simplifies your life and lifts your spirits.

But this kind of freedom isn't really free—it comes with a cost. For starters, Jesus paid dearly for this freedom. The price was his death on the cross. His resurrection became his ultimate freedom—and the reason this kind of freedom is offered to you. Yet there's still a cost for you. The price is simply everything. It's up to you to hand your entire life to God—to entrust all to him, believe in him, study his Word, and know his truth. When you pay that everything price, which is actually pretty small compared to what you receive in return, you will experience real freedom. Because you know God's truth, you are set free.

My Prayer

Dear God,
I want your truth in my life. I'm willing to pay the price—to surrender all to you—so that I can have your real freedom.
Amen.

> ## Stone
> *for the Journey*
>
> **When I know God's truth, I become free.**

Final Word

But when he, the Spirit of truth, comes, he will guide you into all truth. He will not speak on his own; he will speak only what he hears, and he will tell you what is yet to come.

John 16:13 NIV

A Slave to Sin

Words from the Rock

I tell you most solemnly that anyone who chooses a life of sin is trapped in a dead-end life and is, in fact, a slave. A slave is a transient, who can't come and go at will. The Son, though, has an established position, the run of the house. So if the Son sets you free, you are free through and through.

John 8:34–36 Message

A slave is someone who doesn't get to exercise their own will. The master calls the shots, and the slave must simply comply with the master's decisions. Now if the master is God, being a slave is a good thing, because God has only the slave's best interests at heart and would ask them to do only what would help them, not hurt them. But what if the slave's master is evil? What if the slave is being bossed around by sin?

That's what Jesus is talking about here. He's explaining how sin can become a master over you until it almost seems that you have no will of your own. You can be enslaved to deception—it might start with a small lie, but soon it becomes a habit, and before long you can't stop lying. You can be a slave to addictions, whether it's food or computer games or drugs or sex. You know you're a slave when your energy and resources are focused on a behavior that's hurting you, when you no longer control the activity but instead the activity controls you. While you're immersed in it, you are deceived into thinking you enjoy it. But later you are full of regrets, and it feels like you have no choice, like you're trapped. That's being a slave.

So how do you escape that kind of slavery? How can you get out of that trap? Only Jesus can set you free. And that won't begin until you accept the truth by being honest with yourself and openly admitting that you're enslaved to a particular sin. Then you need to ask God for help in surrendering all parts of your life, including that sin area. Maybe God will show you some practical steps to take, like joining a support group or a fitness club. But it's only God's truth (and your acceptance of it) that will set you free. And then you will be really free.

My Prayer

Dear God,
I don't want to be a slave to sin. Help me to be honest—really honest—and to welcome your truth into my life. Then show me the steps to take so I can be free.
Amen.

Stone
for the Journey

God's truth will set me free from the slavery of sin.

Final Word

> You are tempted in the same way that everyone else is tempted. But God can be trusted not to let you be tempted too much, and he will show you how to escape from your temptations.
>
> 1 Corinthians 10:13 CEV

68

God at Work

Words from the Rock

It is not this man's sin or his parents' sin that made him blind. This man was born blind so that God's power could be shown in him. While it is daytime, we must continue doing the work of the One who sent me. Night is coming, when no one can work. While I am in the world, I am the light of the world.

John 9:3–5 NCV

Jesus's disciples have just asked why a man was born blind. They live in an era where physical disabilities or health problems are often associated with sin. So it's natural for them to assume that blindness was the result of sin, and if a person was born blind, perhaps that meant the parents' sin was the reason. But Jesus firmly tells them they are wrong, and then he says something remarkable—that the reason for the man's blindness was to reveal God's power.

That answer must have surprised his disciples. How was it possible that a person born with a handicap could make God look good? It seemed more likely that a person born with something like blindness would shake his fist at God for cursing him with that kind of hardship. In fact, that's the same attitude of some people today. They see someone suffering and ask why God would do that. They blame God for everything that seems to be wrong with the world.

Jesus says these problems and challenges are actually opportunities for God to show what he can do. He's saying that our weaknesses and defects are God's chance to strengthen us, to grow us up, or even to heal us. First we have to realize that we need God's help, and then we need to bring our hardships to him. After that, we need to step back and trust him to work, and once he does, we need to be willing to tell others about what he's done.

My Prayer

Dear God,
Help me to see my personal hardships and challenges as your opportunity to shine in my life. I want to trust you with everything.
Amen.

Stone
for the Journey

God can use my weakness to show his strength.

Final Word

The mind of sinful man is death, but the mind controlled by the Spirit is life and peace.

Romans 8:6 NIV

Blinding Pride

Words from the Rock

> Jesus said, "For judgment I have come into this world, so that the blind will see and those who see will become blind."
>
> Some Pharisees who were with him heard him say this and asked, "What? Are we blind too?"
>
> Jesus said, "If you were blind, you would not be guilty of sin; but now that you claim you can see, your guilt remains."
>
> John 9:39–41 NIV

Why would you pretend to be something you're not? Why would you deny an area of weakness in your life? Would it be because you wanted others to think you were better than you were? Would it be because of pride?

Pride kept the religious leaders and the hypocritical Pharisees from seeing who Jesus really was and that he'd come from God. In fact, pride blinded them. Would they admit they were blind? Of course not. They denied having a problem, insisting that everyone else, including Jesus, needed help. The Pharisees were like, "We can see just fine, thank you very much." They were so sure of themselves that they probably thought their spiritual eyesight was 20/20. Yet they were totally blind. Jesus came to heal the sick and to make the blind see, but if people denied their blindness, like the Pharisees did, how could Jesus possibly heal them?

If we let pride rule us (like the Pharisees) and claim we're "just fine, thank you," Jesus can't help us. Our denial not only keeps us from being healed, it keeps us from God. It's only when we can admit our weaknesses, confess our blind spots (which we all have), and ask God to help us that we can be healed.

My Prayer

Dear God,
I know I have blind spots and that pride can drive me into denial. Help me to confess my weaknesses and to come to you for healing. Amen.

Stone
for the Journey

I will not let pride separate me from the truth and from God's healing.

Final Word

Doing wrong is fun for a fool, but living wisely brings pleasure to the sensible.

Proverbs 10:23 NLT

Attention!

Words from the Rock

*I tell you the truth, anyone who sneaks over the wall
... rather than going through the gate, must surely be a
thief and a robber! But the one who enters through the
gate is the shepherd of the sheep. The gatekeeper opens
the gate for him, and the sheep recognize his voice and
come to him. He calls his own sheep by name and leads
them out. After he has gathered his own flock, he walks
ahead of them, and they follow him because they know
his voice. They won't follow a stranger; they will run from
him because they don't know his voice.*

John 10:1–5 NLT

When Jesus told this parable, people were confused but interested. He'd definitely hooked them with a story that was suspenseful and intriguing. But what did it mean? Who were the thieves and robbers? And why were they sneaking over the wall and stealing the sheep? Really, it made no sense to the listeners. Yet Jesus had gotten their attention, and for a short while he just left them hanging there, wondering.

A lot of spiritual things come at us like that. Something hits us from out of the blue—usually in the form of an everyday incident. It could be something good like an unexpected award. Or it could be something tragic like the sudden death of a loved one. Something occurs that reaches into our lives, grabs us, and shakes us. It gets our attention, but we're not quite sure what it means. Often we don't know how to react. We don't realize that God wants to get our attention so he can show us something. Maybe we too are just left hanging there, wondering.

In this parable, which Jesus explains more fully in the next section of Scripture (which is in the next devotional), it's not hard to guess that Jesus is the shepherd, especially since he's used that metaphor before. But it's still not clear who the thieves and robbers are, or who the gatekeeper is. Mostly Jesus wants us to know that when we feel confused or even blindsided, we need to remember that he has the help and answers we need. When we understand who he is, we learn to rely on him. We look to him for direction and comfort, and we trust him to lead us to safety.

My Prayer

Dear God,
I know that sometimes it takes something difficult to get my attention. Help me focus on you and trust you to get me where I need to go. Amen.

Stone
for the Journey

God needs to get my attention so he can lead me.

Final Word

I pray to you, LORD! You are my place of safety, and you are my choice in the land of the living. Please answer my prayer. I am completely helpless.

Psalm 142:5 CEV

71

Our Entrance

Words from the Rock

*I tell you the truth, I am the gate for the sheep.
All who came before me were thieves and robbers.
But the true sheep did not listen to them. Yes, I
am the gate. Those who come in through me will
be saved. They will come and go freely and will
find good pastures. The thief's purpose is to steal
and kill and destroy. My purpose is to give them
a rich and satisfying life.*

John 10:7–10 NLT

Now Jesus has the full attention of his listeners, and he begins to explain his parable about the sheep, the thieves, and the gate. First he says that the thieves and robbers came before him. It's easy to assume he means the religious leaders who never really cared for the people they were supposed to be serving. Instead of encouraging people to seek God, the Pharisees would trip them up with long lists of ridiculous rules, and then when people couldn't comply with the rules, the Pharisees would demand payment (sacrifices) from them. It was a lot like stealing.

But the new twist in this parable is that Jesus not only calls himself the shepherd, but he tells us he's the gate as well. Jesus is saying that he's our entrance—we must go through him to be saved and to reach God. So not only will he lead us where we need to go, he will also be the actual doorway, gate, portal, entrance, and so on, that will allow us passage from one side to the other. Once we accept him, we walk through that entrance and we're welcome to come and go freely. He will take care of our needs, and our relationship with him will be fulfilling and life changing.

Jesus paints a lot of word pictures for us, giving us image after image of what he's like so we will get it, so we will hold on to who he is and remember it. He calls himself the Bread of Life, the Living Water, the Light of the World, the Good Shepherd, and more. All are invitations to connect to him, to participate in the life he offers us. And when we accept his invitation to pass through him (as the gate), we are immediately transported to the best that life has to offer.

My Prayer

Dear God,
Thank you for inviting me to go through Jesus to reach you. I know the only reason you can give me this free ticket is because you willingly paid the price by laying down your life. I don't want to take that for granted.
Amen.

Stone
for the Journey

Jesus is my entrance to God's very best for me.

Final Word

I have told you all this so that you may have peace in me. Here on earth you will have many trials and sorrows. But take heart, because I have overcome the world.

John 16:33 NLT

Good Shepherd

Words from the Rock

I am the good shepherd. The good shepherd sacrifices his life for the sheep. A hired hand will run when he sees a wolf coming. He will abandon the sheep because they don't belong to him and he isn't their shepherd. And so the wolf attacks them and scatters the flock. The hired hand runs away because he's working only for the money and doesn't really care about the sheep.

John 10:11–13 NLT

Jesus continues to expound on his role as the Good Shepherd. He distinguishes himself from the sort of sheepherder who's not doing a good job—aka the hired hand. This is a guy who took the job probably as a last resort and couldn't care less about the sheep. The hired hand probably doesn't count the sheep at night, he certainly doesn't know their names, and if there's real danger (like a wolf), he will run off to protect himself and let the sheep take care of themselves. He's only in it for the money.

Again, that was a description of many of the religious leaders of that day. Unfortunately, there are still "shepherds" like that nowadays—people in church leadership who don't really care about the congregations they're being paid to serve. They're just in it for the money.

The good news is that Jesus is your Good Shepherd. Even if you should fall victim to a bad shepherd at some point in time (and most people do eventually), that is in no way a reflection on Jesus. In fact, it can simply be a reminder that there really is only one Good Shepherd, and that's Jesus. The more you get to know your Good Shepherd, the more you'll learn to recognize Jesus's voice, and the better you'll become at knowing what's true and what's not. You won't be led astray by a bad shepherd.

My Prayer

Dear God,
Thank you for giving me my Good Shepherd.
Help me to know his voice and to respond
quickly when I hear it.
Amen.

Final Word

> The LORD is good, a strong refuge when
> trouble comes. He is close to those who
> trust in him.
>
> Nahum 1:7 NLT

Stone
for the Journey

I will tune
my ears into
the voice
of my Good
Shepherd.

73

All for Us

> *I am the Good Shepherd. I know my own sheep and my own sheep know me. In the same way, the Father knows me and I know the Father. I put the sheep before myself, sacrificing myself if necessary. . . . This is why the Father loves me: because I freely lay down my life. And so I am free to take it up again. No one takes it from me. I lay it down of my own free will. I have the right to lay it down; I also have the right to take it up again. I received this authority personally from my Father.*
>
> John 10:14–15, 17–18 Message

What's the greatest gift anyone can give? Jesus tells us it's the ultimate sacrifice—to give up a life for someone else— and that's exactly what he's going to do. He will give all he has to give so we can have all he's promised us. It's no small thing. He surrenders his life so we can have eternal life. What a gift! Yet it's a gift that so many take for granted. Or worse, they reject it.

Maybe we take Jesus for granted because we really aren't so very different from sheep. Imagine a young man who has always wanted to be a shepherd. He practiced herding lambs as a child. He's honed his rock-pitching and spear-throwing skills (to scare away predators), and he's gotten into great shape so he can easily keep up with the sheep. He's even researched the best grassy slopes and cleanest streams. He finally gets his shepherding job and takes it very seriously. He always counts the sheep. He gives them names. He tends to their wounds. He even sings them to sleep at night.

But one dark night, a hungry lion decides to attack the herd. As the lion approaches the sleeping sheep, the shepherd throws rocks and spears at it, and finally, just in the nick of time, he tackles the lion. He manages to kill the beast with his knife, but in the midst of the battle the shepherd himself is killed. The sheep continue sleeping, unaware of what's just happened, with no idea of the price of their safety.

Jesus doesn't want you to be like a dozing sheep, oblivious to what it cost to protect you. Instead, he wants you to come to him, spend time with him, and be like the happy sheep, answering quickly when you hear your shepherd's voice.

My Prayer

Dear God,
I don't want to be like one of those sleeping sheep. I want to always appreciate the price you paid by allowing Jesus to die for me. Thank you for giving your all for me.
Amen.

Stone
for the Journey

Jesus gave his life so that I could have life.

Final Word

And I heard a loud voice from the throne saying, "Now the dwelling of God is with men, and he will live with them. They will be his people, and God himself will be with them and be their God."

Revelation 21:3 NIV

Safety Zone

Words from the Rock

I told you already, but you did not believe. The miracles I do in my Father's name show who I am. But you don't believe, because you are not my sheep. My sheep listen to my voice; I know them, and they follow me. I give them eternal life, and they will never die, and no one can steal them out of my hand. My Father gave my sheep to me. He is greater than all, and no person can steal my sheep out of my Father's hand. The Father and I are one.

John 10:25–30 NCV

Jesus is responding to some of the "educated" Jews who are questioning him for the umpteenth time. Jesus probably knows that they don't really want answers and that they're not actually seeking the truth. It's clear from the previous verses that they're more interested in slamming Jesus than anything. In fact, they've just accused him of being demonized or insane. Their goal is obvious—they want to put him down.

When people put others down, it's usually because they hope to make themselves look bigger or better. In this case, these guys probably want to appear scholarly and superior to the onlookers, some of whom actually believe Jesus and want to hear more of his teachings. Jesus, just like his Father, does not waste anything. He uses this as an opportunity to teach about who he really is.

He makes it clear that the guys hassling him are not his sheep (his followers). If they were, they wouldn't be saying such nasty things to him. They wouldn't be so cynical and mean. Jesus points out, once again, that his sheep listen to his voice because they know him and he knows them. He also makes it clear that his sheep will be protected. In essence, they're in a safety zone. No one is going to be able to come in and hurt them.

Jesus promises his sheep (and us) eternal life, and he assures us that as long as we remain in his safety zone, no one can steal us away—not even cruel people who would attempt to fill our heads with lies. We remain safe with Jesus because God is in control and because he and Jesus are one.

My Prayer

Dear God,
I realize that when people put you down, it's because they don't know you. I'm so thankful I know you! And I'm thankful that you'll protect me from those who would try to steal my heart from you.
Amen.

Stone
for the Journey

I am safe because God knows me and I know him.

Final Word

Though I am surrounded by troubles, you will protect me from the anger of my enemies. You reach out your hand, and the power of your right hand saves me.

Psalm 138:7 NLT

Relationship Reflection

Do not believe me unless I do what my Father does. But if I do it, even though you do not believe me, believe the miracles, that you may know and understand that the Father is in me, and I in the Father.

John 10:37–38 NIV

*I*t's really amazing how many chances Jesus gives the Pharisees and religious leaders to believe in him. Despite the fact that they are cruel and demeaning—even accusing him of blasphemy, which is the same as hating God—and despite the fact that they are plotting to kill him, Jesus continues to speak the truth to them. And here's the good news: a few of them actually got it. Oh, it didn't really sink in until after Jesus was killed and rose from the dead, but eventually a few of them figured it out, and you can bet they were sorry for how they'd treated him.

Jesus is telling the Pharisees that they *shouldn't* believe him—unless he does what the Father does and reflects a clear image of who God is. Of course, all Jesus does is represent God's love and mercy, and a lot of his followers already get that. But it's interesting that he says this to the Pharisees. It's almost like a challenge to them. Maybe it was reverse psychology.

Maybe Jesus is trying to remind us about our actions too. Could he be telling us that sometimes we don't act like we really believe him? And when we don't act like a believer, why should anyone think we belong to God? We should be able to see God at work in each other. If we don't, we might need to wonder why. Not that we should judge each other, but if a person claims to be a Christian and yet acts completely opposite of that, it could be that there's a connection problem.

A connected relationship with God miraculously changes who we are. That's because God transforms how we think and how we interact with others. Qualities like love and forgiveness begin to flow more naturally through us, and people around us begin to notice these changes. That's what Jesus is saying: "Look at my life and you'll see that the Father and I are one." He wants you to be able to say the same.

My Prayer

Dear God,
Help me to reflect who you are to those around me. I know I need to be tightly connected to you to become more like you. Help me to be who you want me to be so I can reach out to others.
Amen.

Stone
for the Journey

When I keep my eyes on God, his love reflects through me.

Final Word

> Don't forget to help others and to share your possessions with them. This too is like offering a sacrifice that pleases God.

Hebrews 13:16 CEV

Confidence

76

Words from the Rock

There are twelve hours of daylight every day. During the day people can walk safely. They can see because they have the light of this world. But at night there is danger of stumbling because they have no light.

John 11:9–10 NLT

This seems like such an obvious statement. Of course it's easier to walk during the daylight hours, and yes, you might stumble around in the darkness of night. So?

When Jesus says this to his disciples, it's in response to their concern for his safety. He has just informed them that they'll be traveling to visit a sick friend. Their destination is the same place where the religious leaders recently attempted to get Jesus put to death by stoning. His disciples cannot believe Jesus is willing to return to that town. Isn't he concerned for his safety? Yet his answer to them is fairly nonchalant and seems almost irrelevant—he's talking about walking in the daytime versus walking at night. What is he saying? What does it really mean?

Jesus is simply saying it's not nighttime yet, but he's not talking about physical nighttime. He's talking about spiritual nighttime, a kind of darkness that's coming when it will seem like all the lights have gone out. He's talking about the time that's coming when he will be arrested, beaten, put to death, and in the tomb for three days. Those will be some very dark days for everyone. But Jesus knows it's not time for that yet, so he's not the least bit worried about his safety. His confidence is in God—and God's perfect timing. He knows that he's in his Father's hands. And he's comfortable with that. It's like walking somewhere on a warm, sunny day, when all is well.

It should be no different for us. When we remain in God's will, we can confidently walk in the light too. No fear. Sure, there might come dark times, just like there were for Jesus, but we'll always have that light to guide us. Even when we're surrounded by darkness and all we can see is that small light at the end of the tunnel, we know which direction to walk, and in time we'll make it to the other side.

My Prayer

Dear God,
I want to remain in your will. Please show me how to be better at doing that. Then help me to walk confidently in your light.
Amen.

Stone
for the Journey

God's light reassures me that I'm walking in his will.

Final Word

For I hold you by your right hand—I, the LORD your God. And I say to you, "Don't be afraid. I am here to help you."

Isaiah 41:13 NLT

Sneak Preview

77

Words from the Rock

I am the resurrection and the life. Those who believe in me will have life even if they die. And everyone who lives and believes in me will never die.

John 11:25–26 NCV

Jesus says this to his friend Martha, but his words are for everyone. Martha is grieving the death of her brother, Lazarus, but Jesus is reassuring her that Lazarus will be fine. Her natural assumption is that Jesus means Lazarus will be fine in the afterlife, but that's not very comforting to her right now while her brother's death is so fresh in her mind. Several days ago, while Lazarus was still alive, she'd hoped Jesus would arrive in time to heal him.

But Jesus has something else in mind. Something far bigger than Martha or anyone else can imagine. After Lazarus has been dead and in his tomb for four days, Jesus miraculously raises him from the dead. This miracle is unlike anything Jesus has done up to this point, and people are stunned and amazed. As a result, many of them become true believers in Jesus! But a few doubters run off to tattle this news to the Pharisees.

What the people don't fully grasp is that this miracle is a like a sneak preview of what God is going to do with Jesus before long. Jesus will soon be killed and laid in a tomb, but three days later God will miraculously raise him from the dead. Jesus wants to prepare his followers for this by leaving this vivid memory of Lazarus in their minds. He wants them to get that he is the resurrection and the life, and whoever believes in him will have eternal life!

My Prayer

Dear God,
Sometimes it's hard to grasp that Jesus died and rose from the dead, but I do believe it, and because of that miracle, I believe I can live forever too. Thank you!
Amen.

Stone
for the Journey

The gift of eternity is mine because of Jesus.

Final Word

All of us who are still alive will be taken up into the clouds together with them to meet the Lord in the sky. From that time on we will all be with the Lord forever.

1 Thessalonians 4:17 CEV

78

Priorities

> *Leave her alone. She did this in preparation for*
> *my burial. You will always have the poor among*
> *you, but you will not always have me.*
>
> John 12:7–8 NLT

*J*esus is defending his friend Mary. She has just done a very generous thing, and one of the disciples criticizes her. Ironically, it's the same disciple who will later betray Jesus by revealing his whereabouts, which leads to Jesus's arrest and murder. That betrayer is Judas Iscariot, one of the more "educated" disciples, and the one who handled the finances for the group. But in the end, Judas sells out Jesus for money. Obviously, Judas and Mary are opposites—he frets over finances, whereas she gives freely. Their priorities couldn't have been more different.

Mary gives something to Jesus that's worth far more than the price Judas is paid to betray Jesus. She pours out a very expensive perfume that's sealed in an alabaster box. Only wealthy people had such things, and usually they were saved for a person's burial. Mary probably has no idea that Jesus will soon be killed. She simply does this act out of love. Jesus is more important than anything to her. She willingly breaks open her beautiful box, pours this precious fragrance on Jesus's feet, then dries his feet with her long hair. It's a gesture of true devotion and pure love. Yet Judas derides her for it. Instead of trusting Jesus, Judas is worried about paying the bills, so he complains that it would be better to sell the perfume and give the proceeds to the poor. Again, a difference in priorities.

Jesus knows what Judas is thinking and what he's planning, but instead of calling him out, Jesus commends Mary for her gift. He says it's for his burial, saying they will always have the poor, but he will soon part from them.

This is a reminder for us as well. Jesus doesn't want us to focus on doing good things for others more than we focus on loving him. Out of our love relationship with him will come good things. It's all about priorities. Mary got it. Judas did not. How about you?

My Prayer

Dear God,
I want my love for you be the most important thing I do. I know if I put you first, everything else will fall into place. Please help me to keep my priorities straight.
Amen.

Stone
for the Journey

I commit to love God above all else.

Final Word

I love you, O LORD, my strength.

Psalm 18:1 NIV

Total Trust

79

Words from the Rock

The time has come for the Son of Man to receive his glory. I tell you the truth, a grain of wheat must fall to the ground and die to make many seeds. But if it never dies, it remains only a single seed. Those who love their lives will lose them, but those who hate their lives in this world will keep true life forever.

John 12:23–25 NCV

Jesus is predicting his death, and the day is getting closer. He uses the image of a grain of wheat. Now if you look at a grain of wheat, it doesn't look like much, but it has the potential to produce a whole lot more grain. In fact, over a period of years, one single grain could produce an entire crop—millions of grains. To do this, the grain must die. It has to go back into the earth, and the hard shell that protects the grain has to be broken and deteriorate so germination begins. After that the grain can actually grow into a plant.

Likewise, Jesus knows he has to die and come back to life so his followers can become firm in their faith and go out and tell others. He's like that one grain that falls to the ground and dies but then rises again to produce more grains (more believers), which over the course of time will number into the millions. Jesus trusts God his Father implicitly (to the point of laying down his life) in order to bring life to others.

Jesus takes this a step further by telling his disciples they need to have the same attitude about themselves—they need to trust God enough to be willing to give up their hold on their own lives and follow him. He tells them that if they love their lives, they will lose them. All except Judas take his words seriously because they trust Jesus and love him more than life. In fact, ten of them will be killed for their faith. But their deaths will inspire others to believe, and like the seed that dies, they will become part of the miracle of millions coming to faith. That is ultimate trust.

But Jesus's words aren't only for his disciples. He knows that if we love our own lives more than we love him, we'll ultimately lose our faith—and him. Because he doesn't want to lose us, he encourages us to love him with all we have, even unto death, and he knows that takes total trust.

My Prayer

Dear God,
I probably won't have to physically lay down my life for you, but help me to have the kind of total trust that allows me to love you with 100 percent of my being. I want to love you more than I love my own life.
Amen.

> **Stone**
> *for the Journey*
>
> **I trust God enough to love him more than anything in this life.**

Final Word

Those who obey God's word truly show how completely they love him. That is how we know we are living in him.

1 John 2:5 NLT

80

Devoted Disciples

Words from the Rock

Anyone who wants to be my disciple must follow me, because my servants must be where I am. And the Father will honor anyone who serves me.

John 12:26 NLT

Again Jesus is talking to his disciples about total commitment here, telling them they must follow him and stay with him wherever he goes. He's aware that his death is just around the corner now, but he also knows that his disciples won't be killed with him—their time to die hasn't come yet. So what does he mean? It seems that he's trying to convey that, even after his death and resurrection, they can still have a relationship with him.

Naturally, the disciples don't get this. Not yet. But Jesus is trying to reassure them that they can continue to be with him and to serve him even though he'll be gone. And because he's Jesus and God's Son, he'll be able to deliver on that promise.

That promise isn't only for the disciples who were with him that day. He invites anyone to follow him and to become his disciple. So what is a disciple, and how do we become one? Disciples are ones who *discipline* themselves to become students and devoted imitators of a person they love and admire. Disciples conform themselves to their leader and are willing to change how they think and live in order to serve and be more like that person.

Jesus wants all of his followers to become his devoted disciples. He wants us to spend time with him, learn from him, and imitate him in how we love and forgive others. He wants us to obey him and be completely sold out to him. He promises that when that happens, the Father will honor us.

My Prayer

Dear God,
Teach me how to be your disciple. Show me ways that I can follow you and be with you. I want you to change me into someone like you. Amen.

Stone
for the Journey

I commit myself to being a devoted disciple.

Final Word

Tune your ears to wisdom, and concentrate on understanding. Cry out for insight, and ask for understanding. . . . Then you will understand what it means to fear the LORD, and you will gain knowledge of God.

Proverbs 2:2–3, 5 NLT

Children of Light

For a brief time still, the light is among you. Walk by the light you have so darkness doesn't destroy you. If you walk in darkness, you don't know where you're going. As you have the light, believe in the light. Then the light will be within you, and shining through your lives. You'll be children of light.

John 12:35–36 Message

Jesus has already made it known that he's the Light of the World. His disciples totally get this by now, not only in their heads but in their hearts as well. For more than three years, they've been experiencing Jesus's form of light up close and personal. Surely they remember what it was like before Jesus walked into their lives. Most likely their world was a dark and hopeless place. And thanks to the state of the Jewish religion at that time, they had probably given up on ever being united with God. They probably just went about their daily tasks, focusing only on what they needed to survive, to eke out a living—day in and day out, drearily trudging along.

When Jesus befriended them, it must have been the brightest day of their lives. And as they listened to his teachings and witnessed his miracles, it must have gotten even brighter. They were no longer hopeless. They had a purpose, and it all revolved around their relationship with Jesus.

But then he tells them that he's going to be killed and he'll no longer be with them on earth. Do you think they feel the darkness creeping back into their lives? Do they realize they're about to go through a brief period of darkness? That's what separation from Jesus feels like—cold, lonely, empty, heavy, depressing, confusing . . . darkness. Hope dies, the heart grows weary, life loses its color and its purpose, and we begin to stumble.

Fortunately for the disciples, that darkness would last only three days, but it must have felt like forever. Perhaps that time was a vivid reminder to them that they never wanted to live in the darkness again. Who would?

You don't have to live in the darkness either. Jesus promises that when you believe in him, his light will shine right through you. And what happens when Jesus's light is in you? You can see without stumbling. You can get where you're going without getting lost. And others can look at you and see God.

My Prayer

Dear God,
Please shine your light through me. I don't want to live in darkness—not ever! I need your light to show me where to go and how to live, and to bring warmth and color and life.
Amen.

Stone
for the Journey

Jesus's light gives me life.

Final Word

> Never again will night appear, and no one who lives there will ever need a lamp or the sun. The Lord God will be their light, and they will rule forever.

Revelation 22:5 CEV

God's Light

82

Words from the Rock

Whoever believes in me is really believing in the One who sent me. Whoever sees me sees the One who sent me. I have come as light into the world so that whoever believes in me would not stay in darkness.

John 12:44–46 NCV

Jesus has a short amount of earthly time left, and he really wants to drive some things home. Yes, he's said things very similar to this before, but he knows his disciples (and everyone else) don't always get the real meaning the first time they hear it. In fact, that's why his disciples memorized his words, so they could keep them in their hearts and think on them later. Then they could share these life-giving words with others after Jesus was gone, and they could eventually write them down for future believers to hear and hopefully to memorize as well.

Again Jesus wants to make it crystal clear that when we believe in him, we believe in the Father. He and God are one. You can't have one without the other. You love Jesus, you love God. You serve

Jesus, you serve God. They go hand in hand—there's no separating them. Jesus wants us to know that he's connected to the Father, and we are connected as well because of him. Nothing stands between us and God.

In Jesus's day, the religious leaders drove a wedge between people and God. They set up a legal barrier that made it difficult for people to know who he was. But Jesus tore down that barrier by saying, "You see me, you see God." No more middleman.

Once again Jesus announces that he is the Light of the World, a light sent down from heaven to help us. When we're linked with Jesus, we don't live in darkness anymore. As a result, we have no reason to be stumbling around. If we do stumble, it might simply be a reminder that we're not letting God's light shine down on us as much as he'd like—as much as we need it to.

My Prayer

Dear God,
Thank you for sending Jesus so I can have a relationship with you that will last forever. Thank you for your light. I welcome it into my life.
Amen.

Stone
for the Journey

When I see Jesus, I see God.

Final Word

For I am convinced that neither death nor life, neither angels nor demons, neither the present nor the future, nor any powers, neither height nor depth, nor anything else in all creation, will be able to separate us from the love of God that is in Christ Jesus our Lord.

Romans 8:38–39 NIV

83

Words of Life

Words from the Rock

As for the person who hears my words but does not keep them, I do not judge him. For I did not come to judge the world, but to save it. There is a judge for the one who rejects me and does not accept my words; that very word which I spoke will condemn him at the last day. For I did not speak of my own accord, but the Father who sent me commanded me what to say and how to say it. I know that his command leads to eternal life. So whatever I say is just what the Father has told me to say.

John 12:47–50 NIV

If a guy is starving and you offer him food, but he says "No thanks" and then dies of starvation, would you be to blame? By the same token, if a girl is dying of thirst and you offer her water, but she refuses to drink and then dies of dehydration, would you be to blame? Would their deaths be your fault? Could a judge convict you as a murderer? Of course not! You tried to help them, but they refused your help. They brought their deaths upon themselves.

It's not any different when Jesus offers us the words of life. If we reject his words, if we refuse to listen and believe, isn't it our own fault if we never receive eternal life? Jesus says he didn't come to judge the world. Just the opposite—he came to save the world. That means *everyone* in the world. His desire is that every single person who inhabits the planet will hear his words, and that every single person will receive them for what they are—words of life.

But he can't force anyone to do that, and he won't judge anyone for rejecting his words. That's not his job. Besides, he doesn't need to judge anyone, because those of us who reject his words of life seal our own fate. Just like the guy who refuses food or the girl who refuses water, each of us is responsible for the negative consequences of a bad decision—our own death. Jesus gives all of us lots of chances, right down to our last dying breath, to rethink that decision. He doesn't want anyone to miss out.

My Prayer

Dear God,
Thank you for giving me your words of life.
Please help me to always cling to them, believe
in them, and share them with others.
Amen.

> **Stone**
> *for the Journey*
>
> **Jesus's
> words fill me
> with life.**

Final Word

*I have told you these things so that you will be filled
with my joy. Yes, your joy will overflow!*

John 15:11 NLT

84

Servant Heart

Words from the Rock

Do you understand what I was doing? You call me "Teacher" and "Lord," and you are right, because that's what I am. And since I, your Lord and Teacher, have washed your feet, you ought to wash each other's feet. I have given you an example to follow. Do as I have done to you. I tell you the truth, slaves are not greater than their master. Nor is the messenger more important than the one who sends the message. Now that you know these things, God will bless you for doing them.

John 13:12–17 NLT

Jesus is God—God come to earth—to be light and life and truth, and to show us the way to God's kingdom, where he rules and reigns forever. Yet Jesus gets down on his knees and washes his disciples' dirty feet.

In Jesus's day, it was customary to have guests' feet washed when they came to visit, but it was a job performed by the least of servants or slaves. The purpose of foot washing was twofold. First, it was good etiquette and a way to honor guests. Secondly, people wore sandals and walked on dusty roads, so their feet were dirty, and having them washed was simply good hygiene and a way to keep extra dirt out of the home. Even so, it wasn't the kind of task that servants were eager to do.

But Jesus tells his disciples, who are clearly uncomfortable seeing him down on his knees scrubbing their grubby toes, that he's doing this as an example. He's leaving them another vivid image—something to remember when he's gone—about how important it is for them to follow his example by being servants to each other.

Jesus was a slave to love—he came to serve. He put everyone's needs above his own, even to the point of dying on the cross. The reason he did this was simply because he loves us. He served out of a pure heart of love. And he wants us to imitate him by serving those around us. Maybe this means helping someone else to get ahead instead of pushing your way to the top. Or it could be listening to someone who needs a friend. If you ask, God can show you, and if you're willing, God can put you to work.

My Prayer

> Dear God,
> Thank you for loving me so much that you lowered yourself to serve me by going to the cross. Increase my love for you and others so I can imitate your servant's heart.
> Amen.

Stone
for the Journey

I learn to serve by imitating Jesus.

Final Word

> *Always set a good example for others. Be sincere and serious when you teach. Use clean language that no one can criticize. Do this, and your enemies will be too ashamed to say anything against you.*
>
> Titus 2:7–8 CEV

85

Full Disclosure

Words from the Rock

I am not saying these things to all of you; I know the ones I have chosen. But this fulfills the Scripture that says, "The one who eats my food has turned against me." I tell you this beforehand, so that when it happens you will believe that I AM the Messiah. I tell you the truth, anyone who welcomes my messenger is welcoming me, and anyone who welcomes me is welcoming the Father who sent me.

John 13:18–20 NLT

Jesus previously implied that one of his disciples—one of the men he has loved and served—will betray him, causing him to be arrested and eventually put to death. In fact, that is about to happen. Judas Iscariot is planning to betray Jesus for thirty pieces of silver, yet he's sitting at the table eating with Jesus, listening to him talk, and acting like nothing is wrong.

Now Jesus, rather than calling Judas onto the carpet and pointing him out as a low-life, conniving jerk, simply makes a full disclosure to the other disciples by reminding them that long ago the prophets predicted all this would happen. He wants to make things perfectly clear so that when Judas does what he's about to do, the other disciples will remember Jesus's words and understand why it happened like that. Jesus doesn't want to leave them in the dark about these events, and he wants Judas's betrayal to be just one more thing that assures the disciples and everyone else that he really is who he says—the Messiah, God's Son, their salvation. No surprises. Full disclosure.

Jesus also wants his disciples to know that he doesn't categorize them with Judas. He knows who they are, and he trusts them with the message he's given to them. He knows they'll be faithful with his message even after he's gone, and he tells them that his Father will be so pleased with them that he'll welcome them into his kingdom.

In the same way, God will welcome you when you share his message with others. He'll also partner with you by showing you unique opportunities right there in your everyday life. It all starts with a willing heart.

My Prayer

Dear God,
Thank you for showing yourself to me. Please write your words on my heart and shine your light through me so those who see me will see you at work in me.
Amen.

Stone
for the Journey

When I reveal who God is, I become his messenger.

Final Word

The world and its desires pass away, but the man who does the will of God lives forever.

1 John 2:17 NIV

86

Love's Brand

> *I give you a new command: Love each other. You must love each other as I have loved you. All people will know that you are my followers if you love each other.*

> John 13:34–35 NCV

Jesus has already made many strong statements about love. He's told us to love our neighbors the same way we love ourselves. He's even told us to love our enemies. As simple as those commands might sound, they're not easy. Loving others as much as you love yourself doesn't come naturally. And loving your enemies—well, that's downright hard.

Now Jesus is giving a new commandment that really takes the idea of loving others up a few notches. He challenges his disciples (and all who would follow him) to love people the same way he loves people. Think about it—the way Jesus loved the world was to give up everything he had by leaving heaven and coming to earth. He became a servant to everyone by helping and healing and teaching. Then he showed the ultimate sacrifice of love by laying down his life so we could all be forgiven and received into his kingdom. Love just doesn't get any better than that. It's no small thing that he wants us to follow his example by loving others like he did.

How do we do that? First of all, we have to invite Jesus, the author of love, to lead us. That means we make sure that above all else, we're receiving his love and loving him in return, because it's out of our relationship with him that we can begin to love others. Then we need to remember the love basics that Jesus taught. "Love your neighbor as yourself" (Matt. 22:39 NIV) means loving others (including our enemies) in the same way we want to be loved—the same way Jesus loves us. That means our love is unconditional, kind, honest, energetic, selfless, genuine, humble, generous, thoughtful, and so on. And don't forget that love always goes hand in hand with forgiveness. Love without forgiveness isn't love.

When we live out this forgiving kind of love, it's like we're wearing a brand—a brand that shows we belong to God!

My Prayer

Dear God,
Thank you for loving me! I want to love others like that. Help me to learn from you so my love will remind people of your love.
Amen.

Stone
for the Journey

When I love like Jesus, people see God at work.

Final Word

> *Love is kind and patient, never jealous, boastful, proud, or rude. Love isn't selfish or quick tempered. It doesn't keep a record of wrongs that others do. Love rejoices in the truth, but not in evil. Love is always supportive, loyal, hopeful, and trusting.*
>
> 1 Corinthians 13:4–7 CEV

87

Second Chances

Words from the Rock

Simon Peter asked Jesus, "Lord, where are you going?"

Jesus answered, "Where I am going you cannot follow now, but you will follow later."

Peter asked, "Lord, why can't I follow you now? I am ready to die for you!"

Jesus answered, "Are you ready to die for me? I tell you the truth, before the rooster crows, you will say three times that you don't know me."

John 13:36–38 NCV

*R*emember when Peter answered Jesus's question "Who do you say I am?" exactly right? Jesus was so pleased that he told Peter, "I'll build my church on you." Now Jesus is telling him that, before morning comes, Peter will deny him not once, but three times! Poor Peter. How do you think that made him feel? Or maybe he didn't believe it. After all, he loved Jesus with his whole heart. How was it possible he could deny him three times? Yet Jesus was right—Peter did deny him three times. Sure, it was out of fear that he too might be arrested and tortured, but the fact remains.

The real reason Peter denied Jesus was because he was operating on his own strength, and that was not enough, especially when times were beginning to get hard. But later on, after Jesus's death and resurrection, Jesus would return to give Peter and the rest of his followers a form of super strength (aka the Holy Spirit). After that, Peter would not only remain totally faithful to Jesus, he would also become that spiritual rock Jesus had described before—and an important part of the foundation of the early church.

Jesus gives second chances, and third chances, and as many chances as we need because he knows that, like Peter, we will blow it. We might even deny knowing Jesus when we're backed into a corner. But if we return to Jesus, like Peter did, and if we allow Jesus to empower us with his Spirit, our faith will grow stronger, and we'll learn from our mistakes. Then Jesus will be able to use us in ways we can't even begin to imagine.

My Prayer

Dear God,
I don't ever want to deny you, but if I do, please remind me that you give second chances.
Please strengthen my faith by the power of your Holy Spirit so I can serve you wholeheartedly.
Amen.

> ## Stone
> *for the Journey*
>
> **When I need it, God gives a second chance.**

Final Word

If we confess our sins, he is faithful and just and will forgive us our sins and purify us from all unrighteousness.

1 John 1:9 NIV

88

Home Sweet Home

Words from the Rock

> *Do not let your hearts be troubled. Trust in God;*
> *trust also in me. In my Father's house are many*
> *rooms; if it were not so, I would have told you. I*
> *am going there to prepare a place for you. And if*
> *I go and prepare a place for you, I will come back*
> *and take you to be with me that you also may be*
> *where I am. You know the way to the place where*
> *I am going.*
>
> John 14:1–4 NIV

These have to be some of the most reassuring words ever spoken. Jesus gives a priceless promise that can carry us through the tough times. He gives us his word that we'll be with him in heaven someday. But first he tells us not to let our hearts be troubled, which basically means don't be afraid and don't worry. Jesus knows we'll all face some hard times, times when it will be easy to be consumed with fear and worry. But he tells us to trust God and to trust him, and then he tells us a little about the place he's getting ready for us.

Jesus doesn't go into much detail about what heaven will be like. But consider the vast creativity of God and how beautifully he's made the earth, and consider some of our favorite places on this planet (like amazing mountains, gorgeous beaches, mystical rainforests, or tropical paradises). If we multiply those natural wonders many times over (because heaven will totally outshine earth), we might begin to have a tiny speck of an idea of how incredible our next home will be.

And the promise doesn't end there. No, Jesus wants us to know that he will personally escort us to this place. How or when this will happen is still a mystery, but it's reassuring to know that Jesus isn't going to leave us dangling between this life and the next. All we need to do is to love, trust, and serve him until that time comes.

My Prayer

Dear God,
Thank you that you have a place waiting for me in your house. I admit that I can't even imagine how great that will be, but I trust you and know I won't be disappointed.
Amen.

Stone
for the Journey

I will trust God for this life and the one that's yet to come.

Final Word

Our bodies are like tents that we live in here on earth. But when these tents are destroyed, we know that God will give each of us a place to live. These homes will not be buildings that someone has made, but they are in heaven and will last forever.

2 Corinthians 5:1 CEV

Way, Truth, Life

Words from the Rock

I am the way, and the truth, and the life. The only way to the Father is through me. If you really knew me, you would know my Father, too. But now you do know him, and you have seen him.

John 14:6–7 NCV

*T*hree rather ordinary-sounding words—*way, truth, life.* Yet when you connect these three little words to Jesus, they become everything. Really, what more do we need?

Jesus is the way. He's going to get us where we need to go. Once we believe in him, it's like we've climbed aboard this incredible ship that will transport us to God. Sure, there could be some rough seas, and it might not always look like he's taking us where we want to go, but he will get us to the right destination. And it'll be a voyage we'll never forget.

Jesus is the truth. We live in a world filled with tricksters. Deception and lies come at us on a regular basis, and sometimes it's hard to know just who's really telling you the truth. Perhaps it's enticing but false claims made by marketing gurus trying to sell their "latest greatest," an enemy posing as a friend, or someone trying to scam us on the Internet. But Jesus is the truth. His love and forgiveness are authentic. We can take him at his word and never be disappointed. He is the real deal.

Jesus is the life. Without Jesus, we're not really living. Oh, we might be breathing and eating and walking, but we won't be truly alive. Jesus is like an incredible life transfusion that restores us and invigorates us to a place where we really engage, where we become passionate, and where we truly experience the fullness of life God planned for us from the beginning. That's really living!

My Prayer

Dear God,
Thank you for being all that I need—the perfect formula. You're the *way* to get me there, the *truth* I can count on, and the *life* that energizes me into action.
Amen.

Stone
for the Journey

Jesus gives me all I need—the way, the truth, and the life.

Final Word

*What you hope for is kept safe for you in heaven.
You first heard about this hope when you believed
the true message, which is the good news.*

Colossians 1:5 CEV

90

Promising Promise

Words from the Rock

> *Believe me when I say that I am in the Father and the Father is in me. Or believe because of the miracles I have done. I tell you the truth, whoever believes in me will do the same things that I do. Those who believe will do even greater things than these, because I am going to the Father. And if you ask for anything in my name, I will do it for you so that the Father's glory will be shown through the Son. If you ask me for anything in my name, I will do it.*
>
> John 14:11–14 NCV

Can you believe that you could do the kinds of things Jesus did during his earthly lifetime? Or even things that are greater? Do you think you could make a blind person see, make a wheelchair-bound person walk, or feed everyone in your school's cafeteria with your brown-bag lunch? It seems unlikely, doesn't it? Yet, as impossible as that sounds, Jesus says it *could* happen—if you believe in him.

Incredibly, it did happen for Jesus's disciples. After his death and resurrection, he returned to give the disciples his Holy Spirit, and suddenly miracles were happening left and right. Everyone who witnessed these things, including the disciples, was totally blown away. Thousands of people came to faith. It must have been fun.

Still, you have to wonder, can that possibly happen now? Is this promise really meant for everyone? You have to put it in perspective. Jesus says many times that his promises aren't limited to his disciples or followers more than two thousand years ago; they're for everyone throughout the ages.

So the conclusion has to be that miracles *could* happen. In fact, there are many modern-day miracles. Some of the most amazing ones happen in struggling third-world countries, where people are more desperate and therefore their faith might be stronger. Even so, we need to remember and cling to this promise: Jesus says that whatever we ask in his name, he will do. The key here is to ask in his name—ask according to who he is, according to his will. That means we have to be tightly connected with him, letting his life be lived out in us. That's when anything can happen!

My Prayer

Dear God,
I want my faith to grow, and I believe you can do great things through me. That means I need to stick close to you, and I need you to live your life in me.
Amen.

Stone
for the Journey

With God's help, I can do anything.

Final Word

Surely your goodness and unfailing love will pursue me all the days of my life, and I will live in the house of the LORD forever.

Psalm 23:6 NLT

Melody Carlson is the award-winning author of around two hundred books, many of them for teens, including the Diary of a Teenage Girl series, the TrueColors series, and the Carter House Girls series. She and her husband met years ago while volunteering as Young Life counselors. They continue to serve on the Young Life adult committee in central Oregon today. Visit Melody's website at www.melodycarlson.com.

START STUDYING THE BIBLE FOR ALL IT'S WORTH!

Maybe you've heard this before: "Jesus is the Rock." But what does it really mean? And what does it mean to you personally? Find out in this 90-day devotional on the words of Jesus from bestselling author Melody Carlson.

Revell
a division of Baker Publishing Group
www.RevellBooks.com

Available wherever books are sold.